Knowing God's Will

Biblical Principles of Guidance

M. Blaine Smith

Foreword by
Richard C. Halverson

InterVarsity Press
Downers Grove
Illinois 60515

To my wife, Evie

I wish to convey my deepest thanks to my wife for
typing the original and revised manuscripts
and for her constant encouragement and support
in numerous ways. Also, my very special thanks go
to Dr. George Scotchmer, the session and people of
Memorial Presbyterian Church, St. Louis, who provided
most of the time during which this book was written.

© 1979 by Inter-Varsity Christian Fellowship of the United States of America

InterVarsity Press is the book-publishing division of Inter-Varsity Christian Fellowship,
a student movement active on campus at hundreds of universities, colleges
and schools of nursing. For information about local and regional activities, write
IVCF, 233 Langdon St., Madison, WI 53703.

Distributed in Canada through InterVarsity Press, 1875 Leslie St., Unit 10,
Don Mills, Ontario M3B 2M5, Canada.

All biblical quotations, unless otherwise indicated, are from the Revised Standard Version of
the Bible, copyrighted 1946, 1952, © 1971, 1973, and are used by permission.
ISBN 0-87784-610-3
Library of Congress Catalog Card Number: 78-24756

Printed in the United States of America

18   17   16   15   14   13   12   11   10   9   8
93   92   91   90   89   88   87

Foreword

While attending seminary, I was a member of what we called "Deputation Teams." Various churches in the Northeast area of the country invited us for special services—usually youth conferences on weekends. As part of this weekend there was nearly always a question-and-answer time during which we seminary students would respond.

Invariably one question asked had to do with the will of God— "How can I know God's will for my life?" or some variation of that theme. In the course of college and seminary I had developed a simple little formula which had been gleaned from several sources. With a great degree of confidence I would prescribe this formula after which the matter was settled as far as I was concerned. Unhappily for those who raised the question, this was not so. The formula proved to be artificial and mechanical, and it lacked biblical insights which came much later for me.

On reading this book, I wished that I had been able in those seminary days to give the instruction so ably presented here.

Blaine Smith writes on the subject with extraordinary maturity and careful attention to the Scriptures. As I read his manuscript it seemed that he had thought of everything. He begins by facing and eliminating the most common misunderstanding relating to the subject. Briefly and incisively he puts away false notions held by many and often propagated with devastating effect.

His treatment of the relationship between divine sovereignty and human freedom and responsibility is excellent, as is his distinction between moral and nonmoral issues.

Here is a presentation on knowing God's will that is carefully thought through, well annotated, comprehensive, exceedingly practical and compellingly readable.

Richard C. Halverson
Washington, D.C.
January 1979

Defining
the Problem

I

A
Serious
Concern

1

"IF THERE IS A SERIOUS CONCERN among Christian students today, it is for guidance. Holiness may have been the passion of another generation's Christian young men and women. Or soul winning. Or evangelizing the world in their generation. But not today. Today the theme is getting to know the will of God."[1]

I would agree fully with Joseph Bayly's claim. But I would go one step further. I believe this concern for guidance is not only typical of Christian students but is really the central concern of most adult Christians today. As a pastor I find that the good majority of people seeking my counsel are seeking help in understanding God's will, and I find the typical Christian is confused over how to know God's will.

This confusion is surely due in part to the incredible diversity of choice we face as twentieth-century believers. Christians of previous centuries usually found their major choices in life parentally or culturally determined. But today we have a freedom of choice and opportunity that makes decisions considerably more complex, and confusion over God's will is the natural by-product for the Christian.

No Lack of Advice

The confusion is also nurtured by a lot of popular ideas floating around Christian circles about knowing God's will. So many well-meaning people offer simple and foolproof solutions to guidance. If you will just apply these principles, they say, then the will of God will be obvious. But unfortunately you find that the principles are not always so easily applied in concrete situations.

And worst of all, the simple and foolproof solutions sometimes contradict each other. One person says, "Love God and do what you wish," while another insists, "To find God's will you should deny your desires." One teacher says, "God's will is normally the most logical alternative," while another points out, "Abraham 'went out not knowing whither he went,' so God's will may seem illogical to you." One counselor says, "God's will is known through your intuition," while another argues, "Feelings are misleading; God directs through rational thought processes."

Advice abounds for people seeking God's will. Some promote the practice of "putting out a fleece." Others, especially in charismatic circles, stress the role of supernatural guidance through signs, visions or prophecy. Still others claim that God's will is best found through certain chain-of-command relationships. And a surprising number of Christians actually encourage the use of secular forms of guidance, such as astrology, Ouija boards, séances and palm reading.

All in all, it is no wonder the typical Christian is baffled by the prospect of finding God's will. In some cases the results of this confusion can be tragic. A young woman came to me convinced God had told her to kill herself. Assuming God was speaking to her through her impulses, she took her suicidal urges as divine guidance. Although her case is clearly extreme, it dramatizes the problems that can arise in this area.

A more typical case is that of a teacher friend of mine. Although he was having success as a teacher, he was frustrated by the lack of a clear calling to the teaching profession. "The Bible declares that St. Paul was commanded by God to be an apostle," he said. "My problem is that I don't feel commanded by God to do anything!" Like so many Christians today he was perplexed over how God's call to a particular profession might be known and wondered why he did not receive a call as unmistakable as Paul's. Lacking this clear sense of calling, he found his work regrettably mundane.

I could share many other examples from my own experience of people confused over God's will, as well as plenty from my own life. But my guess is that you can supply plenty of your own examples. You probably need little convincing that a problem exists here. I am sure you would agree that it is an understatement to say that there is value in studying what the Scriptures teach in this area.

The Task Ahead

My purpose in this book is to study the biblical principles of guidance, in order that the reader might develop a solid biblical foundation for making personal decisions. I should warn you in advance that I will not end up with a pat formula or two into which you can plug all your complicated decisions and get an immediate answer to God's will. God does not expect our decision making to be any easier than it is for nonbelievers, in fact we may even find it more difficult. But I am convinced that a thorough understanding of the biblical teaching on guidance can considerably reduce confusion over God's will.

In chapter two I will define two terms which are basic to our study—*complex decisions* and *the will of God*. I want to point out some distinctions which will be helpful to our whole discussion.

In part II, I will deal with the question most basic to guidance: What is God's responsibility, and what is mine? It is my belief that God himself takes the initiative in guidance. Therefore, much of the anxiety suffered over the possibility of missing God's will is unjustified, for it is God's responsibility to lead us. But I must also stress that if we take our relationship with God seriously, we will seriously strive to understand and follow his will. He allows us this responsibility for the sake of our growth in Christ. This responsibility amounts to four things: having an attitude of willingness to do God's will; praying for guidance; studying Scripture; and using our minds to make logical, intelligent decisions. In the end, knowing God's will boils down to making a rational decision.

I will examine in part III two popular approaches to guidance which tend to distract us from rational thinking—supernatural guidance and inward guidance. While we should not close ourselves off to the possibility of supernatural guidance, and while we should have a proper respect for intuition, neither of these approaches should take precedence over sound thinking.

Personal desires, abilities, circumstances and the counsel of others are often the providential indications of God's will. I will discuss how to evaluate each of these factors in part IV.

Finally, I will try to give you a couple of concluding illustrations which will help tie all the points together.

You could call this study a *wholistic perspective* on knowing God's will. I have tried to deal systematically with the teachings of the whole Bible on guidance, hopefully touching on the major issues raised by the subject. I have also taken a wholistic view of the Christian life. Too often as believers we view the Christian life in extreme terms. On the one hand are those who feel that self-denial must characterize the lifestyle of the believer. On the other hand are those who think that the bent of the Christian life should be toward personal fulfillment. In reality, *both* these factors should play an important role, and a mature Christian perspective includes both self-denial and self-affirmation. Understanding the relationship between these two is a vital part of understanding how God makes his will known. I will deal with this issue at various places in our study.

As you begin this book, you may be tempted to skip to the chapter that seems most interesting. But I believe the study will be most meaningful if the chapters are followed in order. They build on one another to some extent, and some of the later chapters would be difficult to understand fully without the concepts established in the earlier ones.

It is my hope and belief that you will find this study helpful in your personal search to know God's will. I trust it will lead you to a deeper experience of joy in the Lord.

Key
Concepts

2

OUR FRUSTRATION in knowing God's will often begins for two reasons. First, we make the mistake of thinking that God's will should be sought in the same way for all different types of decisions. Actually, different decisions require different approaches to God's will. Second, we are not really clear what we mean by the will of God. There are actually two basic concepts implied by the phrase *will of God* which need to be understood before we can intelligently discuss how God's will can be known.

In this chapter, then, we will look at the various types of decisions which we make as Christians, and we will note some key distinctions. Then we will examine what is meant by the phrase *will of God*. These preliminary discussions will provide an important background to the rest of our study.

Moral and Nonmoral Decisions
It has been helpful to me to make a distinction between two basic types of decisions we face as Christians. On the one

hand, we have what we can call straightforward *moral decisions*. These are the ones to which a single, clear moral principle can be applied. They include, for instance, decisions about stealing, killing or extramarital sex. In every case the decision has to do with a specific area of behavior which requires the same type of response every time. The moral principle tells us what that response should be. In this sense, once a particular moral principle is understood, God's will in that area becomes a matter of application. We do not have to rethink the problem every time it arises. If I know that God does not permit adultery, for instance, I do not have to waste mental energy deliberating whether he might be leading me to have an affair with my neighbor's wife. The simplest moral decisions are straightforward, clear and direct, because a single biblical principle applies directly to them.

On the other hand, there are those personal decisions to which moral principles have no relevance. Straightforward *nonmoral decisions* deal with our choice about actions which have no moral implications at all. For example, no biblical principle applies to whether I wear a blue shirt today or a yellow one. This is a very simple decision and one which is nonmoral in character.

Complex Decisions

Perhaps the easiest way to conceive of the relationship between moral and nonmoral decisions is as though they form a continuum (see illustration). At one pole are the simplest, most obvious moral choices, and at the other pole are the simplest nonmoral decisions. As we move from left to right on the continuum, our decisions become less clearly settled by a single moral principle and our liberty of choice increases. We encounter more complicated moral decisions, such as abortion, the question of a Christian's response to war and so on. These are issues which require careful deliberation and a delicate balancing of two or more moral principles.

Next we come to what have traditionally been called "gray

The Shades of Decision Making

area decisions." These have to do with areas of moral behavior where the Bible clearly leaves the individual Christian some freedom of choice. In Paul's day this included questions of eating meat (Rom. 14:2) and observing certain holidays (Rom. 14:5). In the twentieth century Christians have often been concerned with matters such as smoking, drinking, dancing or gambling.

Then we come to choices which I call *complex decisions.* These are important personal decisions which have to do with more than merely matters of moral behavior. Complex decisions include major questions such as what profession to choose, what college to attend, whether or not to marry and where to go to church. They also include decisions about priorities: how should you spend your time and money? In general, questions such as these cannot be resolved simply by applying moral principles to them. In most cases we are left with a good deal of freedom of choice. These are unique decisions which may require very different responses from time to time and from person to person.

This does not mean that complex decisions have no moral aspects to them. Certainly most of the important decisions we confront in life involve moral issues in one way or another.

But what I mean is that moral principles will not finally settle these questions. Moral principles may simplify them or narrow the area of focus. For instance, if I am wrestling with God's will for a job position, I can rest assured that he does not want me to become a palm reader or manager of a brothel. But no moral principle will give me the final insight into God's will if I am trying to decide between becoming a doctor or a lawyer, a bookkeeper or a welder, a pastor or a missionary. As a result, such decisions are often complicated, since they cannot be conveniently settled by reference to moral principles alone.

In this book we will be interested purely in the question of knowing God's will for complex decisions. This is the area of decision making that usually causes the most difficulty and where we most often experience confusion over God's will. Usually when we talk in Christian circles about needing guidance from God, we are talking about his leading for this sort of decision.[1] Therefore, when we use the term *guidance* in this book, we will always use it in this sense. (Much of what we will say will also have relevance to making a gray area moral decision. There are, however, certain additional guidelines for the gray area decision.[2])

I hope that these distinctions will be helpful to you, the reader. Much of the value in drawing them lies in helping us understand the role the Bible should play in our decision making. Since the Bible is our prime source of moral principles, we should expect to find the answer to a moral decision in the Bible. At times a single moral principle will give the answer clearly and directly. In other cases a weighing of various principles will lead to the right answer. But since complex decisions cannot be resolved by moral principles alone, we should not expect the Bible to provide us with final answers. A person seeking God's will for a profession, for instance, should not expect to find a biblical passage telling him or her to become an accountant. A woman considering whether to marry a particular man should not expect to find a verse which finally settles the question.

I realize this goes against the grain of much popular thinking on guidance. It is often taught that the answer to any
conceivable decision is given in the Scriptures. We just need to
find the right passage. This causes some people to end up in a
frustrated search for a biblical principle which will conclude
their decision. Others turn their search for guidance into pure
superstition by seeking guidance from irrelevant words or
passages. A classic example is the man who decided to marry a
woman named Grace on the basis of the verse, "My grace is
sufficient for thee." Many people blindly open the Bible, place
their finger on a verse and take guidance uncritically from the
verse.[3] I love the illustration Paul Little gives of this
approach:

> Some people treat the Bible as a book of magic. You have
> probably heard of the fellow who opened the Bible and put
> his finger down on the phrase, "Judas went out and hanged
> himself." This did not comfort him very much, so he tried
> again. And his finger fell on the verse, "Go thou and do
> likewise." That shook him terribly, so he tried it one more
> time, and the verse he hit on was "And what thou doest, do
> quickly."[4]

Only when we recognize the futility of such an approach to
guidance can we really be free to seek God's will in a mature
and responsible way.

This does not mean that the Bible should play no role in
making complex decisions. It is through the Bible that we
learn principles of guidance which tell us how to seek God's
will, and throughout this book we will be looking at these principles. Also, through the Bible we learn moral principles
which must not be sidestepped in discerning God's will. We
will, in fact, devote an entire chapter to looking at the positive role of Scripture in guidance, as there is a good deal more
that needs to be said about it. For now, however, we are simply
saying that we should not expect to find the final answer to a
complex decision magically revealed in the words of Scrip-

ture. We should avoid the crystal-ball approach to the Bible which looks for easy answers to difficult decisions and seeks to escape from our God-given responsibility for careful decision making.

God's Plan and God's Wish

Another distinction which is very helpful to make is that between God's future plan and his present wish. One of the most highly emphasized teachings in Christian circles today is that God has designed a unique plan for the life of each believer. "God loves you and has a wonderful plan for your life" is law one of Campus Crusade's *Four Spiritual Laws,* the world's most popular evangelistic tract. This teaching is, of course, an important one, worthy of emphasis, for it deepens our trust in God's capacity to guide us. But unfortunately many Christians reach the unjustified conclusion that they need to discover something of God's future plan for their lives in order to assess his will for each present decision.

Interestingly, however, the Scriptures nowhere teach that knowledge of the future is necessary or even helpful for intelligent decision making.

To begin with, whenever the New Testament refers to our responsibility for knowing or doing God's will, the Greek term used for *will* is always *thelēma,* which generally implies not God's resolute intention but simply his wish or desire, which requires our cooperation for its fulfillment.[5] When Paul states, for instance, "this is the will of God, your sanctification: that you abstain from unchastity" (1 Thess. 4:3), he is not talking about something God plans to do regardless of our cooperation. He is stating a wish God has for our behavior which we can choose to obey or not.

Another Greek term sometimes interpreted as *will (boulē),* indicates God's immutable plan which will be carried out regardless of our cooperation.[6] Thus Jesus was delivered up "by the deliberate will [*boulē*] and plan of God" (Acts 2:23 NEB). But nowhere does the New Testament suggest that we should seek knowledge of God's *boulē* in making personal decisions.[7]

Furthermore, nowhere else does the New Testament counsel us to seek any knowledge of our own future. It might be argued that Paul urges this when he encourages the gift of prophecy.[8] But many scholars feel that this gift refers not to foretelling the future but to teaching.[9] Even if prophecy indicates prediction, I do not believe that Paul implies that we should try to predict our own future through this gift. We will note in chapter eleven that Paul sees the gifts of the Spirit not for personal edification but rather for the benefit of the body of Christ. Whatever he means by prophecy, he means a gift through which we can minister to other Christians. It would be wrong to see this gift as some sort of magical tool for simplifying our own decisions.

While the New Testament gives no encouragement to seek knowledge of the future, the Old Testament vehemently warns against this activity. Statements are numerous throughout the Old Testament condemning fortunetelling.[10] And when Saul, king of Israel, sought knowledge of his future through a fortuneteller, God actually slew him for doing so (1 Sam. 28—31; 1 Chron. 10:13-14). There is no denial that fortunetelling may sometimes provide reliable insight into the future. Thus Saul gets a correct prediction of his death through the witch (1 Sam. 28:9) and Balaam the diviner gets an accurate notion of God's intention to bless Israel (Num. 22:7-12). The point is that we have no business looking into the future; such knowledge can only be harmful.

We can suggest many reasons why knowledge of the future could be harmful to us. First, it could be paralyzing. This was precisely Saul's experience when he consulted the witch. He learned through her séance that his doom was near, and this knowledge was so frightening that it immobilized him (1 Sam. 28:20). And we can guess that in the large majority of situations into which God leads us we would shrink back from fear if we had full knowledge of the difficulties ahead. How many, for instance, would willingly get married if they had a full preview of all the challenges awaiting them? God leads us as much by information he withholds as by information he gives!

Second, knowledge of the future could stifle our moment-by-moment obedience to God. If we knew for certain what God intended to do with our lives, we would begin to feel as though we had God "locked in"—that no disobedience on our part would prevent God from carrying out his plan.

Third, such knowledge could also stifle our moment-by-moment faith and trust in God. If we knew for certain what God was going to do in the future, we would have no opportunity for the kind of faith required when we are forced to trust him each moment for fresh guidance.

Fourth, knowledge of the future could stunt the growth of the intellectual faculties God has given us for decision making. Being spiritually "spoon-fed," we would not develop our rational abilities to make responsible decisions.

Finally, if it had no other detrimental effect upon us, such knowledge would probably add a dimension of boredom to our lives. Knowing what the future held would cause us to lose the sense of curiosity which adds a continual element of anticipation to our existence. Being guided step by step is surely a much more exciting experience than having before us an elaborate blueprint of the future.

It should be clear, then, that knowing God's future plan would not normally be good for us. Predicting the future should not be our concern as Christians, and we may be freed from the anxiety of thinking we need to know the future to understand God's will for the present.

We do not deny that there might be rare occasions when God would wish to reveal the future to someone, and we certainly do not deny that God has the power to do this. But Scripture gives us no reason to expect this would happen frequently, nor that the average Christian would ever experience such knowledge. We should assume that, apart from God's giving an unsolicited revelation of the future, such knowledge would be harmful to us.

One further point deserves mentioning. Since we should not normally expect knowledge of the future from God, we should beware of thinking that the guidance we receive from him is a revelation of his future plan for us. This is a crucial point. Too often when we discern God's will for a present decision we make the leap to assuming we have learned his future intentions for us. The man who is led by God to spend time with a certain woman, for instance, may jump to the conclusion that God intends for them to get married. It is, however, normally wrong to reach any final conclusions about God's will beyond his leading for the present moment.

It is presumptuous to say, for instance, "It is God's will for me to be a missionary in India next year." The most that can reasonably be said in faith is, "It is God's will for me *to move in the direction of* becoming a missionary in India next year." In other words, while we can be confident of God's will for a present decision, we should not assume this tells us what the implications of that decision will be. God may be leading me to move in the direction of becoming a missionary to India not because he wants me to end up in that position, but because he wants me to gain training for another vocation that I would not have pursued otherwise. Only if and when I finally end up as a missionary on Indian soil can I finally say without qualification that God wills for me to do such work.

We should not, of course, hesitate to move toward the goal we sense God leading us toward merely because we realize we might never reach that goal. If this were our attitude we would be paralyzed, and God could never guide us anywhere. Many times, in fact, we will find that the goal God has placed in our minds turns out to be his actual target. But we should be careful of jumping to conclusions about the future from knowing about the present. Ultimately all projections of God's plan should be carefully qualified with "if the Lord wills" (Jas. 4:15).

All in all, then, we can see that we should neither seek

knowledge of God's future plan nor assume that God might be showing us that plan through his guidance for a present decision. If in a rare instance God would wish to reveal the future to us, we must trust that he would make this revelation unmistakably clear. Apart from this, we should assume that the only guidance we need for a decision is simply a knowledge of his present wish.

Moving On

By now you should have a better idea of what sorts of decisions we will look at in this book. We will limit our attention to those decisions which are not indisputably settled by moral principles. We call these complex decisions. These cannot be resolved simply through a clever use of Scripture. God's will in them must be sought outside of the Bible, but in light of biblical principles of guidance.

We want to know how to find God's present wish for these decisions, not his future intentions. This is the most we can legitimately ask when seeking the will of God.

In the chapters which follow we will consider how we should seek God's present wish for our complex decisions. But now that we have made it clear what we mean by that, we will avoid using such academic terminology and will simply talk about knowing God's will. Hopefully these distinctions will make the discussion more enlightening and our personal search for God's will more focused.

God's
Responsibility
for Guidance—
and Ours

II

The
Promise
of Guidance

3

THE SUBJECT OF GUIDANCE should really begin with God—what is his role in the whole process? Unfortunately, many popular discussions on guidance leave us feeling as though guidance depends on our ability to figure out God's will. We fail to realize that guidance ultimately is *God's* problem. We have reason to feel secure.

I do not in any way want to argue that there is no responsibility on the human side in guidance. In fact, the majority of this book is devoted to looking at that responsibility. But first, we need to come to grips with the kind of attitude in which this responsibility is to be carried out—an attitude of tremendous assurance that God himself takes the initiative in guiding the person who is open to being directed by him. I cannot possibly emphasize this point strongly enough.

If we are really honest, we have to admit that we experience a lot of anxiety in this area. We fear that if we do not discern God's will carefully enough in some key part of our lives we will miss it. When I was single, for instance, I remember feeling like I was walking a spiritual tightrope in various dating relationships. I would be on edge, wanting to know God's will for each relationship, fearing that if I missed a signal here or a sign there, I would miss God's plan and forever forsake the chance to be married to the woman of his choice.

But the more I understand about the biblical teaching on guidance, the more I am convinced that this sort of anxiety is largely misplaced. I see an overwhelming emphasis in the Bible on a God who takes the responsibility to guide us in spite of our confusion over his will.

Just Following Along

If we merely study the many instances in Scripture where God gives supernatural guidance, for example, we discover a very intriguing fact. In most cases God intervenes unexpectedly and gives a person guidance even when no request has been made for it. In other words, God goes "out of his way" to make sure the person has adequate knowledge of his will in order to do it.

We see God doing this when he calls various great leaders in biblical history. Consider, for instance, Moses, who was tending sheep for his father-in-law when God called him to deliver the people of Israel from slavery in Egypt (Ex. 3). Or Saul, who in looking for some lost asses was led to Samuel who annointed him king (1 Sam. 9—10). Or David, who was tending the flock and because of his age was not at first included with his seven brothers when they were "interviewed" by Samuel for the position of king (1 Sam. 16:1-13). In none of these instances did any of these men have the slightest inkling that he was about to be commissioned for an extraordinary leadership task. They were simply doing their duty, carrying out their mundane responsibilities (not even seeking special guidance), when God broke through and revealed his will to them.

Beyond such examples, there are numerous statements

throughout the Bible which point directly to God's sovereign initiative in guidance. But there is probably not a more profound and helpful picture of this role in the Bible than the analogy of God to a shepherd leading his sheep. The analogy of God's care for Israel to a shepherd's care for his sheep is a familiar one in the Old Testament.[1] In the New Testament Jesus is pictured as the Good Shepherd, who compassionately leads like sheep those who choose to follow him. We find this picture developed most extensively in John 10, one of the most inspiring New Testament statements on guidance:

"Truly, truly, I say to you, he who does not enter the sheepfold by the door but climbs in by another way, that man is a thief and a robber; but he who enters by the door is the shepherd of the sheep. To him the gatekeeper opens; the sheep hear his voice, and he calls his own sheep by name and leads them out. When he has brought out all his own, he goes before them, and the sheep follow him, for they know his voice. A stranger they will not follow, but they will flee from him, for they do not know the voice of strangers." This figure Jesus used with them, but they did not understand what he was saying to them.

So Jesus again said to them, "Truly, truly, I say to you, I am the door of the sheep. All who came before me are thieves and robbers; but the sheep did not heed them. I am the door; if any one enters by me, he will be saved, and will go in and out and find pasture. The thief comes only to steal and kill and destroy; I came that they may have life, and have it abundantly....

My sheep hear my voice, and I know them, and they follow me; and I give them eternal life, and they shall never perish, and no one shall snatch them out of my hand." (vv. 1-10, 27-28; see also Heb. 13:20; 1 Pet. 2:25, 5:4; Mt. 9:36.) Throughout this passage Jesus explicitly speaks of taking the sort of responsibility for his followers that a shepherd takes for his sheep. And this responsibility clearly involves guidance: "he calls his own sheep by name and leads them out"

(v. 3); "he goes before them, and the sheep follow him, for they know his voice" (v. 4); "My sheep hear my voice, and I know them, and they follow me" (v. 27). And Jesus further makes a key reference to guidance in verse 9: "If any one enters by me, he will be saved, and will go in and out and find pasture." The concept of eternal life and salvation Jesus presents here implies much more than life after death; it indicates a *quality of life* brought on by the leadership of Christ, which begins the moment one is born of Christ. The reference to going in and out and finding pasture is to a Jewish expression of the time: "To be able to come and go out unmolested was the Jewish way of describing a life that is absolutely secure and safe."[2] Here Jesus indicates the freedom and security a sheep could enjoy under the care of a conscientious shepherd.

There are really two things that make this shepherd analogy a particularly encouraging one for us who are seeking the will of God. The first is the nature of the shepherd in New Testament times.[3] The Palestinian shepherd was known, not only for his compassion toward his sheep, but also for his firm leadership of them. The shepherd was really an autocrat over his sheep, taking absolute responsibility to see that the sheep got from one pasture area to another.[4] And he would take whatever measures necessary to ensure this, short of physically harming the sheep. If a sheep strayed from the fold, for instance, the shepherd might sling a rock toward the sheep, aimed carefully so that it would land directly in front of the sheep. The shepherd was an expert marksman, and while this rock would land very close to the sheep, it would not actually hit it. The sheep, though unharmed, would be startled and would quickly return to the comfort of the fold.[5]

But not only are we given an encouraging statement of God's guidance through the picture of the shepherd, but also through the picture of the sheep. The sheep, of all animals, is known for being exceedingly dumb—a beast with little sense of direction, who can scarcely find the way anywhere without the shepherd. When Jesus wanted to talk of lost people in terms of a lost animal, he spoke of lost sheep, for a sheep when lost is really lost.[6] The sheep is totally dependent upon the shepherd.

What we have, then, is a picture of God's guidance which is extremely comforting. We are reminded that God realizes we are like sheep who have little sense of where we should be going, who experience tremendous confusion over his will. But God takes a phenomenal amount of initiative to guide us in spite of our confusion. Realizing this should bring us tremendous security as we seek to know and to do the will of God.

No Need to Fear

Realizing God's concern for me should free me from the fears that are common to those who seek to know his will. First, I can be free of the fear that God will not give me the information I need to decide within his will. It is easy to fall into the trap of thinking that God is too busy, or too far removed, to be concerned with giving me guidance. He would surely give guidance to the great saints and Christian heroes—those whom he uses to make an obvious mark on the course of history—but it is presumptuous for me to expect the same sort of leading from him. I am simply not that important. Yet to understand Jesus' language in John 10 is to realize that God's guidance is not something reserved only for the Christian "heroes" but a precious gift given to each and every believer. The picture of the sheep certainly depicts not a spiritual hero but an ordinary believer. And Jesus talks about giving guidance to *all* his sheep (v. 4) and makes an explicit promise in verse 9: "I am the door; if *any one* enters by me, he will be saved, and will go in and out and find pasture" (emphasis added).

Second, I can be released from the fear that I might not be able to understand God's will if he does convey it to me. In other words, even if I believe God will give me guidance, I may doubt my ability to understand what he is saying. In my finite understanding I might miss a key signal which would throw me hopelessly off the course of God's will. But when Jesus promises in John 10 that he will lead us, he is promising much more than simply the giving of information. He is promising a shepherd's guidance, which means he will take the full responsibility to see that we get where he wants us to go when we are open to his leading. Where we lack understanding, he will so arrange our circumstances that we still end up doing what he desires. He is simply too big to allow our lack of understanding to keep him from leading us in the path of his will.

Furthermore, I can be free of the fear that a past decison made in faith could later be found to be outside of God's will. As Christians we are notorious for re-evaluating our past decisions. We may be convinced that a certain decision is God's will, but later we discover new information which would have caused us to decide differently, and we conclude that we must have misjudged God's leading. A friend of mine, for instance, recently told me that although he had felt strongly led by God to go to St. Louis, severe job frustrations were now making him think he had misunderstood God's direction in moving there. But if we take God's sovereignty in guidance seriously, we must conclude that such rehashing of past decisions is really unnecessary. It is also impious. I must trust that God allowed me to have the information I needed at the time of the decision and likewise withheld information that might have discouraged me from going where he wanted. Later information may signal a change in direction, but it cannot challenge my original understanding of God's will. God leads as much by information he withholds as by information he gives.

Finally, I can be free of the fear that my sin might ultimately cause me to miss God's plan for my life. Now here I need to back up quickly and draw some strong qualifications to what I am saying. I am talking here about the person who is serious about wanting to do God's will. I find that among such persons there are some who have a deadly fear that their own sinfulness is interfering enormously with God's plan. They worry themselves sick that they will never find the person God wants them to marry or never end up in the profession in which God wants them, because their sin will cause God to reject them from his plan.

I hope it can be seen that this sort of fear is quite unjustified in the person who has a heart toward doing God's will. I think the most beautiful aspect of the shepherd-sheep analogy is that it reminds us vividly that Christ not only guides us in spite of our confusion about his will, but also guides us in spite of our waywardness. Sheep in the Bible are pictured not only as confused animals, but also as wayward animals.

I realize here that we immediately confront a host of theological questions about God's sovereignty versus man's free will and responsibility. If dealt with thoroughly, these difficulties would take us considerably beyond the confines of this book. The minute we begin to deal in this realm, we must realize we are confronting a theological mystery which cannot be fully explained. Yet there are some very practical observations for guidance which can be made.

On the one hand it is clear from the Bible that we are to have a healthy fear about the possibility of our sin interfering with God's will—I am not in any way denying this. It is abundantly clear from Scripture that our sin can and often does cause us to deviate from God's perfect plan. It is clear that our sin always causes us to miss blessings we would have known if we had followed God's will more perfectly. Christians who are indwelt by the Holy Spirit are going to be concerned about the sin in their lives and are going to carry on a lifetime battle with it.

But on the other hand, it is equally clear that we are not to be obsessed with a fear that loses sight of the fact that he who is in us is greater than he who is in the world. In fact, it can certainly be said that if we have a healthy concern about sin in our lives, there is no need for extreme fear. The biblical picture of guidance is one of God's taking the person who has a basic desire for his will and working out a plan in that person's life which is realized to an important extent in spite of his or her weakness and sin. While sin may cause a person to miss some of the blessings of God, it does not throw him or her hopelessly off the path of God's will. We see this illustrated in person after person among the great saints of the Bible in the Old and New Testaments.

What this boils down to is that if our basic disposition is to do God's will in the first place, we may be confident that he will take us to the key points in his plan, even though we may reach them in a wayward manner. While we need always to be doing battle with sin in our lives, the battle should be carried on in a spirit of victory rather than a spirit of defeat. Our search to know and do God's will should be carried out in an attitude of tremendous security, not one of neurotic anxiety.

As we move from here to look at what this search for God's will really involves, I sincerely hope you will keep in mind the points that have been stressed in this chapter about God's initiative in guidance. The remainder of this book will be devoted to looking at what *our* responsibility is in the process of discovering God's will for complex decisions, and as you can see, there is a great deal to be said in this area. Yet we must be careful not to lose sight of the forest for the trees. We must never forget that guidance is ultimately God's responsibility, that he is infinitely more concerned that we do his will than we could ever be, and that he is taking a most gracious initiative to guide us in the path of his will as we are seeking to respond to him.

Guidance for the consecrated believer is not merely a possibility, nor simply a good probability. It is a promise—one of the great promises of the Bible.

Are
You
Willing?

4

NOW THAT IT IS CLEAR what responsibility God takes for guidance, in the next four chapters we will consider our role in the process.

In making a complex decision it is helpful to think of our responsibility as having four basic aspects. First, we have a responsibility to be willing to do God's will in the decision; that is, to strive for an attitude of submission to his will. Apart from this willingness, it is doubtful we will really be able to understand his will or be able to do it. Second, we should spend time in prayer over the decision. In big decisions especially, this is a responsibility that must not be taken lightly. Third, we need to study Scripture with respect to the decision. Fourth, we must use our God-given reason to make an intelligent choice that seems most glorifying to him.

We will look separately at each of these four areas of responsibility. It should be said that these four are really inseparable; we cannot carry out any one of them apart from the others. Yet for the purpose of gaining a mature understanding of guidance, we will find it beneficial to take a separate look at each of these areas and the particular implications each has for our lifestyle as believers.

Being Open to Suggestion

We will begin by looking at the need for willingness to do God's will. It is often thought that our main role in guidance is to try to figure out what God's will is. But without wanting in any way to belittle our responsibility in that area, I must stress that biblically our primary responsibility is not an intellectual but a *volitional* one. Before all else we must strive for an attitude of willingness to do God's will; it is only in the context of such an attitude that we can truly see clearly what God's will is. I am convinced that in the majority of cases the reason Christians experience long-term confusion over God's will is not because his will is not clear enough but rather because they simply do not want to accept it.

Throughout the Bible, for instance, where we see God giving special calls to various people, in almost every case it seems that the person called was willing to do God's will before it was ever revealed.[1] This is clear simply from the fact that most of the time we see the person responding quickly and obediently to God's call. While there are cases where great leaders felt ambivalence about their ability to carry out the call (for example, Moses or Jeremiah), we seldom sense that underneath they were resistent to the call. And it was certainly this underlying attitude of heart which had much to do with God's choosing them for extraordinary tasks.

I do not know of a passage in Scripture that sums up this condition of willingness and its results more succinctly than Romans 12:1-2: "I appeal to you therefore, brethren, by the mercies of God, to present your bodies as a living sacrifice, holy and acceptable to God, which is your spiritual worship. Do not be conformed to this world but be transformed by the renewal of your mind, that you may prove what is the will of

God, what is good and acceptable and perfect."

This passage makes a tremendous promise about the will of God: that we will *prove* the will of God ("what is good and acceptable and perfect" is a modifying clause). The word *prove* in the Greek is a pregnant term for which we really have no good English equivalent. It is the same term used of the process of purifying precious metal in a furnace and testing its strength. In the context of our passage it means that we will live out God's will and discover it through experience. In plain and practical terms, it means we will both know God's will and do it at the same time. We will have the knowledge of God's will that we need along with the spiritual strength to carry it out. This is the promise of guidance we saw in the previous chapter.

But the passage also states two conditions to the promise. The first is given by "present your bodies as a living sacrifice." Paul sees this as a commitment of one's entire being to Jesus Christ, like the commitment made once and for all in marriage.

The second condition is indicated by "do not be conformed to this world but be transformed by the renewal of your mind." The verbs in this statement in the Greek are in a tense which indicates repeated action. The negative side of this condition ("do not be conformed to this world") suggests that we must strive to avoid doing those things we clearly know are against the will of God. The positive side ("but be transformed by the renewal of your mind") tells us that we must be constantly yielding our minds to the control of the Holy Spirit. Here, however, it is important to understand that the word *mind* in Greek is *nous,* which means not just intellect, but also the whole "inner direction of one's thought and will and the orientation of one's moral consciousness,"[2] with a special emphasis upon will.[3]

Paul, more than anything, is telling us that we must constantly strive for an attitude of yieldedness, an attitude of openness to the will of God. If we have that attitude, then, Paul makes it clear that we will both know and do God's will. In short, then, Romans 12:1-2 makes a remarkable statement: *If I am willing to do God's will, I will do it.* This is really the most important point of our study.

In practical terms I believe this willingness really amounts to two things. First of all, I must do what I already know to be God's will. And second, I must be willing in advance to accept whatever alternative God might show to be his will. In order to determine this, I should imagine all the alternatives which could be logical options to a decision. If I know that I would accept any of these if God said to do so, then I may be confident that I am willing to do his will. This does not mean that God will necessarily lead me to choose the least appealing alternative (we will discuss the problem of understanding our desires in chapter ten), but it does mean that I must be willing to accept that option if it is clear God wants me to.

Unfortunately, this is where we too often run into problems. We are intensely curious about God's will. But we have already made up our minds, and we are hoping that his choice will coincide with ours. We are hoping God will rubber-stamp the decision we have already made. Or, while we may be open to certain alternatives, we remain closed to others.

This reminds me of a young woman who came to me for vocational counseling. She desperately wanted to find employment in a particular artistic field which would also give her a unique chance to witness for the Lord. I immediately thought of an opportunity she could pursue in California and suggested it to her. Her reply, however, was most revealing She was sure God would not want her to go to California. It would be too far away from family and friends; she was sure God would want to give her a job in the eastern part of the U.S As we talked, she finally admitted that even if God wanted her to go to California, she simply was not open to making such a move.

Hopefully we can see that when this is our attitude, it is really beside the point to expect God to show us anything Only when we are willing in advance to accept whatever God might want are we in a position where we can hope to prove his will.

What about Motives?

In talking about willingness we must be clear that we are not talking about an absolute purity of motives. It is sometimes implied in popular writings on guidance that it is impossible to know the will of God until we have perfectly pure motives. But such pristine purity is nothing short of a psychological impossibility. I doubt if it is ever possible to do anything as Christians where there is not at least some selfishness of motive involved; this is simply part of the plague of always having the old nature to deal with this side of eternity. And I believe it is simply axiomatic that when Christ leads us to do something, we will almost immediately begin to experience selfish motives for doing the very thing he is calling us to do. The person called to be a missionary, for instance, will almost unavoidably begin to imagine all the praise and honor this sacrificial service will bring from people back home. This is an impossible psychological syndrome out of which to break.

It is precisely here that many Christians with sensitive consciences end up paralyzed. At first they are convinced about a course of direction Christ wants them to take. But then they begin to experience selfish motives, and, try as they may, they cannot get rid of these. So they reach the fateful conclusion: Christ must not be leading them in this direction at all. Satan, I believe, has a field day immobilizing Christians through this sort of introspection.

We need to see that selfish motives are to some extent inevitable. To be sure, we must make every effort to purify our motives, but we must not allow our concern to paralyze us from action that would otherwise seem to be glorifying to God. We should consider our disposition toward God's will more from the standpoint of whether we are willing to do whatever he would ask than from the standpoint of what our motives are.

Here Oliver Barclay makes a helpful suggestion:

> If we are honest we shall never be certain that our motives
> are absolutely pure. We know our own hearts too well. In
> such a decision we must pray for a true objectivity and ask
> God to give us such an overriding desire for his honor and
> glory that we are able to judge aright. But it is no good
> indulging in endless introspection. We must make allow-
> ance for our own selfishness and get on. By all means we
> must pray about it and ask to be given a willingness which
> does not come naturally to us and a fresh love for him which
> makes selfish considerations small. But then we must turn
> to the objective task of seeking out the divine wisdom of the
> matter, determined that, by God's grace, we will obey
> whatever is right.[4]

In short, then, being willing to do God's will is more a matter
of will than a matter of motive.

The Problem Remains

Yet, when all is said and done, having willingness to do God's
will can still be a real problem. I believe we face two problems
in particular here. On the one hand we sometimes simply do
not want God's will in some area of a decision and are quite
aware of it. The young woman who was unwilling to go to
California is a case in point. But on the other hand there is a
more subtle problem we can face, and that is the difficulty
encountered when we think we really want God's will but
underneath have reservations. The classic biblical example is
certainly Peter, who was firmly convinced he would never
betray Christ but then denied him three times. Because of this
possibility I believe we should assume in any major decision
that unwillingness is a problem with which we must deal.

The question, then, really becomes, how do we deal with
unwillingness—either when it is an obvious problem or when
we want to guard against the possibility of being unwilling
when the chips are finally down? Here we raise the most
important question of our study. And we must not minimize

the problem here. Overcoming resistance to God's will is tantamount to changing the will, a most difficult task, as anyone who has tried to renounce a habit will testify. We might even go farther and argue that theologically it is an impossibility for any of us to change our own wills through our own strength.

Fortunately, we will see that there is a practical solution to this problem in the right use of prayer. It is through prayer that we can successfully do battle with an unwilling disposition, to the point of being confident that we are ready to do God's will. We will see that the role of prayer in guidance is rather different from what we may have supposed.

Asking
for
Guidance
5

IT GOES WITHOUT SAYING that prayer plays a vital role in guidance. Few of us walk with Christ for very long without discovering this. Yet I believe that few Christians really understand the nature of the role that prayer should play in guidance. Most think of prayer as necessary simply to petition God to make his will known. But while prayer is important in this respect, its primary purpose in guidance should not be for gaining a knowledge of God's will but rather for gaining the willingness to do it.

We will first look at the role of prayer in asking for knowledge of God's will, as this is still a key area not to be overlooked. But then we will give special attention to the function of prayer in helping us gain the strength to do the will of God.

Praying to Know God's Will
It is always something of a mystery to explain exactly why prayer should be necessary in the Christian life, and theolo-

gians throughout the ages have attempted to do this. If God is sovereign, and if he knows our needs before we even express them to him (as Matthew 6:8 clearly says), then why the need for prayer? C. S. Lewis probably gave the most succinct answer when he said that God could have chosen to do his work on this earth in any fashion he wanted, but he chose in his sovereignty to do it (in part) in response to prayer.[1] Prayer is really for our sake; it is through prayer that God allows us to take responsibility for his work in the most mature and wholesome sense, and it is through prayer that we are allowed the privilege of spiritual growth which can come by no other means.

Regardless what we would say about the "why" of prayer, its necessity cannot be denied. The importance of prayer is underlined throughout every portion of the Bible; so much so that John Calvin, in spite of his great stress upon God's sovereignty, devoted a healthy portion of his *Institutes of the Christian Religion* to prayer. He stated, "we see that to us nothing is promised to be expected from the Lord, which we are not also bidden to ask of him in prayers."[2] Andrew Murray put it even more strongly:

It is in very deed God's purpose that the fulfillment of His eternal purpose, and the coming of His kingdom, should depend on those of His people who, abiding in Christ, are ready to take up their position in Him their Head, the great Priest-King, and in their prayers are bold enough to say what they will that their God should do. As image-bearer and representative of God on earth, redeemed man has by his prayers to determine the history of this earth.[3]

When it comes to the matter of knowing God's will, the Bible makes it clear that we should not presumptuously expect God to reveal it to us. Rather, we have a responsibility to petition him to make his will known. In Joshua 9 we are given a most revealing picture of what can happen when this is not done. The Israelites had experienced recent victories of incredible magnitude—crossing the Jordon, destroying Jericho and Ai.

They had been commanded to destroy the inhabitants of the
land of Canaan, and they were going well about the task. But
the people of a city called Gibeon, near to where the Israelites
were camped, were determined to avoid annihilation, so they
devised a plot to deceive the Israelites into sparing them. They
dressed up in old, tattered clothing and carried dusty, worn-
out provisions, and approached the Israelite camp, telling
them they were from a nation far away. They persuaded the
Israelites to make a treaty of peace with them. Their plot
succeeded magnificently, and the Israelites were completely
beguiled. The Bible makes it clear that there was a plain and
simple reason why God allowed the Israelites to be tricked,
and that was because they did not stop to ask for divine
guidance in the matter. "So the men partook of their provisions, and did not ask direction from the LORD" (Josh. 9:14).

In the New Testament the most explicit command to pray
for knowledge of God's will is given in James 1:5-6: "If any of
you lacks wisdom, let him ask God, who gives to all men gen-
erously and without reproaching, and it will be given him. But
let him ask in faith, with no doubting." James here tells the
believer to pray for wisdom; that is, for God's perspective on
things. Although in the context of the passage James is talking
about wisdom in the face of trials (see vv. 2-4), scholars assert
that "the language employed is so general, that what is here
said may be applied to the need for wisdom in all respects."[4]
"If any of you lack wisdom," is certainly an ironic statement; of
course we all lack wisdom and are in constant need of it.
James, then, tells us that when we lack understanding of God's
will we have a responsibility to ask him to make it plain.

There is no question that a great many of us as Christians do
not begin to take this responsibility seriously enough. In
Affirming the Will of God Paul Little recalls his own experience:

At the Urbana Convention in 1948, Dr. Norton Sterrett
asked, "How many of you who are concerned about the will
of God spend five minutes a day asking him to show you his
will?" It was as if somebody had grabbed me by the throat.

At that time I was an undergraduate, concerned about what I should do when I graduated from the university. I was running around campus—going to this meeting, reading that book, trying to find somebody's little formula—1, 2, 3, 4 and a bell rings—and I was frustrated out of my mind trying to figure out the will of God. I was doing everything but getting into the presence of God and asking him to show me.[5]

Then Little adds, "May I ask you the same question: Do you spend even five minutes a day specifically asking God to show you?" All of us as Christians would do well to take this question to heart. Praying for God's will is a daily responsibility, and one for which the serious Christian must simply make time.

On the other hand I believe there are Christians who actually take this responsibility too seriously. There are those, for instance, who pray incessantly for guidance on mundane matters. Hopefully, it can be seen that if we are to live our lives fruitfully and efficiently for the Lord, it is simply a bad investment to spend much time in prayer over a simple decision. Paul Little again has an apt comment: "God really does not have a great preference whether you have steak or chicken. He is not desperately concerned about whether you wear a green shirt or a blue shirt. In many areas of life, God invites us to consult our own sanctified preferences. When we are pleased, God is pleased."[6]

This does not mean there is anything wrong in asking God briefly for guidance even in small decisions as part of continually practicing his presence. But to spend much time in prayer over them really shows a lack of faith in his capacity to guide. It is a much better approach merely to spend a few minutes in prayer each day asking God to guide all the minor decisions of that day. Then go ahead and apply yourself to the day's decisions in the faith and confidence that God is answering your prayer.

I also believe there are Christians who spend too much time praying for God's will in major decisions. Such praying can all too easily become a cop-out from doing what is very obviously God's will. Or else it can be a sign that we lack faith that God will show us his will. As one friend of mine put it, "I sometimes pray to God to show me his will to the point of unbelief!" In the passage from James quoted above, James says that praying for wisdom must be done *in faith*, and this means believing God will give wisdom once we have prayed for it. To pray importunately for a knowledge of God's will, then, might be a sign of a lack of faith.

It is most interesting that beyond this passage in James, there is no other direct statement in the New Testament telling us to pray for a knowledge of God's will, in spite of the extensive emphasis on prayer. Likewise, in the book of Acts, where we have many examples of prayers, there is only one clear instance of a prayer for God to reveal his will.[7] We must conclude from this that while praying in this area is important, it should not be the burden of our prayer life.

Asking God for wisdom to make decisions is vital, but it should be done in the context of a broader devotional time, where we thank God for his blessings, make requests for the needs of others, confess our sins, and spend time in his Word. When we are faced with a major decision, we should spend a concentrated period in prayer for guidance. Some of this time should be spent petitioning God to make his will clear, but even more time should be spent asking the Lord to give us a heart that desires his will and a spiritual strength to do it. This is the most essential function of prayer in guidance and the area to which we now turn.

Praying for Strength to Do Right
There is one passage which I feel is perhaps the most fascinating and instructive biblical statement on prayer—the Gethsemane passage, where Jesus prays for strength to face his crucifixion.

He began to be sorrowful and troubled. Then he said to them [Peter, James and John], "My soul is very sorrowful, even to death; remain here and watch with me." And going a little farther he fell on his face and prayed, "My Father, if it be possible, let this cup pass from me; nevertheless, not as I will, but as thou wilt." And he came to the disciples and found them sleeping; and he said to Peter, "So, could you not watch with me one hour? Watch and pray that you may not enter into temptation; the spirit indeed is willing, but the flesh is weak." Again, for the second time, he went away and prayed, "My Father, if this cannot pass unless I drink it, thy will be done." And again he came and found them sleeping, for their eyes were heavy. So leaving them again, he went away and prayed for the third time, saying the same words. (Mt. 26:37-44)

In this passage we observe a most intriguing fact. Jesus, the Son of God, experiences a human will different from God's. He has difficulty being willing to do God's will—the very problem we have talked about. As he contemplates the torture of the crucifixion and the agony of bearing the cup of human sin, his human will is understandably resistant. His desire is that he could somehow be spared the agony of the cross. This fact alone—that Jesus experienced emotional difficulty in yielding to God's will—should be tremendously reassuring to us and should encourage us not to be unduly harsh with ourselves when we have a similar problem.

But the passage not only shows that Jesus had this problem—it also shows how he dealt with it. It is *through prayer* that Jesus successfully overcomes the dichotomy between his will and God's. And how he prays is most significant. He begins by confessing his true desires to God: "My father, if it be possible, let this cup pass from me." This certainly shows us the freedom we have—even the mandate—to be brutally honest before God. But Jesus then goes a step further and prays, "nevertheless, not as I will, but as thou wilt." In effect, by praying in this way Jesus was asking God to grant him the willingness to yield to the Father's will above his own. The essence of Jesus' prayer, then, was, "God, grant me the strength to do your will."

It is interesting to note that nowhere in the Gospels do we discover Jesus, for all his emphasis upon prayer, ever praying for a knowledge of God's will. Because Jesus was God, he apparently did not need to pray in this way. But he did find it necessary to pray for willingness; and if Jesus needed to pray in this fashion, it forcibly underlines the need for this kind of prayer in our own lives. When facing a major decision we should see the necessity for spending a concentrated time praying for the strength to do God's will, and we should see this as even more important than praying for a knowledge of God's will.

As I have said before, this is not to imply that praying for knowledge of God's will is unimportant. Unlike us, Jesus knew clearly what God's will was, and he prayed for yieldedness in light of that clear understanding. Our responsibility goes beyond his in that we must also pray for enlightenment. But I believe his example tells us where the emphasis should be in our prayers. And I also believe this truth comes across strongly in the advice Jesus gives his disciples in this passage. Jesus tells them to make the same type of prayer that he was making. He tells them, "Watch and pray that you may not enter into temptation; the spirit indeed is willing, but the flesh is weak." He was, in effect, telling them that apart from doing this they would lack spiritual power. Now what is significant is that the disciples, unlike Jesus, did not know exactly what was ahead; they were expecting a crisis situation, but they were uncertain what choices they would have to make. Yet note that Jesus does not tell them to pray for the knowledge of what God would have them do, but rather for the strength to do it. Jesus knew that their greatest problem would not be knowing what to do but having the strength to carry it out.

And the results, of course, bear Jesus out in a most convincing way. The disciples do not pray; they go to sleep. Then when Jesus is betrayed, they find themselves completely lacking the fortitude to stick with him (Mt. 26:56), even though they had sworn they would never deny him (Mt. 26:35).

The Gethsemane passage, then, strongly suggests that prayer for the willingness to do God's will is necessary in the Christian life. We should pray earnestly for willingness before facing a crisis situation or a major decision, and our prayers for guidance should concentrate more on willingness than on knowledge.

If the Gethsemane passage is not convincing enough, we should also note that in the Lord's Prayer, which Jesus gave us as a model for our daily prayer life, there are actually two petitions which amount to requests for the ability to do God's will: the third petition ("thy will be done") and the sixth ("lead us not into temptation"). Interestingly, these correspond to Jesus' prayer in the garden and the one he told his disciples to make. Thus it is most significant that Christ's model prayer, while including no petition for knowledge of God's will, exhorts us to pray for yieldedness. It is clear that this sort of praying is a necessity for serious Christians. It is central to guidance and basic to gaining the willingness to do God's will. Through praying for yieldedness, we may be confident our decisions are in the will of God.

How Much Prayer Is Enough?

At this point, a practical question arises: Just how much time should we spend praying in this way before making a big decision? In the last chapter we said that willingness to do God's will is a preface to being able to know his will and to having the spiritual capacity to carry it out. And now we are saying that prayer is the key to gaining this willingness. At what point do we know we have prayed enough to be sufficiently willing?

Here it is difficult to give a perfect answer. I believe the only really helpful answer is to say that we must pray until we have reached the point of being reasonably assured that we are open to God's will. Here I stress the word *reasonably*. In most cases it is impossible to know with absolute certainty just how yielded we actually are; even a man with the remarkable maturity of the apostle Paul claimed, "I do not even judge myself" (1 Cor. 4:3). We may have the problem of thinking we are more yielded than we really are, the same problem Peter and the apostles faced in the garden. Or we may have the opposite problem—because the Holy Spirit is working in us, convicting us, we may have an intensive awareness of our sinfulness to the point of thinking of ourselves as more resistant to God's will than we really are. A friend of mine during the last two years has lost over two hundred pounds in a demanding Weight Watcher's program, going from obesity to a very trim figure. Yet she still thinks of herself as fat. In the same way, as we grow in Christ, we may have difficulty shaking off old self-images. The Christian with a scrupulous conscience may pray endlessly for willingness to do God's will and never feel fully assured he or she has attained it.

There are, of course, those times when we are well aware of significant areas of resistance in a decision. If I am considering several professional possibilities, and if I believe there is reason to think God might want me to enter teaching, yet I have closed my mind to that possibility, I can bet that there is some real unwillingness with which I must deal. But if it is merely a case of some vague, nagging doubts about my yieldedness, then I should probably go ahead and make my decision, realizing these doubts are probably more a sign of spiritual health than anything else.

Whatever the case, we should certainly spend a concentrated period praying for guidance before proceeding with a major decision. Just how long that time should be cannot be set down in a rigid formula; it might be fifteen minutes in one case, a day or more in another. There should obviously be some relation to the dimension of the decision and to our ability to concentrate in prayer. But ultimately the time comes when we have to stop praying and go ahead with the decision, trusting that God is answering our prayers and giving us the willingness and wisdom for which we have prayed. This, of course, means a certain risk; yet the element of risk can never be removed from living a life for Christ on the growing edge.

The wonderful fact is that we can take this risk with confidence that we follow a forgiving God who promises to give us the sort of shepherd's guidance we talked about in chapter three. He is able to work even our mistakes into his plan.

Listening

We have stressed in this chapter that praying for guidance is tremendously important for those of us who wish to know and do the will of God. We have noted that we are expected to ask God to show us his will, but not to the point of becoming obsessed with this kind of praying. And we have emphasized that in praying for guidance we need especially to petition God to grant us a desire for his will and the spiritual strength to yield to his will above our own.

You may wonder at this point why our whole stress in this chapter has been on making requests to God. Why has nothing been said about the important matter of *listening* to God in prayer? Is not prayer communication with God, a time when more than anything we quietly listen and gain an understanding of his will? I would hope that you are raising this question.

Actually the whole rest of the book will be devoted to this question, to the matter of listening to God. While we will not talk so much about prayer during the rest of our study, everything we will say touches on communication with God. Keep in mind that any serious effort to discern God's will should always be undertaken in a spirit of prayer or closeness to God. What we will talk about next is how we should endeavor to listen to God in the most mature and responsible sense.

Searching
the
Scriptures
6

UP TO THIS POINT we have stressed the fact that God takes the initiative in guidance and that our main responsibility is to be in close communion with him. If I am willing to do his will, I may feel confident that he will ensure that I walk in his will, even when I feel confused about it. We have stressed that prayer, more than anything, is the channel through which we develop and maintain an openness to the will of God.

Use Your Head
All of this should not in any way suggest that we are to send our minds on vacation while seeking God's will. Someone might logically conclude that if God will guide us whenever we are submitted to him, even though we are confused about his will, then there is really no point in making a mental effort to discern his will. "Why bother?" some might ask. The answer is simple: Scripture clearly tells us that we have a responsibility to seek God's will. We would do well to keep in mind what

the psalmist says: "I will instruct you and teach you the way you should go; I will counsel you with my eye upon you. Be not like a horse or a mule, without understanding, which must be curbed with bit and bridle, else it will not keep with you" (Ps. 32:8-9). Here we see God's promise of guidance coupled with a clear command to use our minds to discern it. While God will guide us with the bit and bridle if necessary, this is not the way he would have us proceed.

I think we can suggest at least four reasons why it is important to use our minds in understanding God's will:

1. *Our need for personal growth.* It is a simple fact that we cannot grow in any area apart from being exercised and challenged. If we merely allowed God to guide us like puppets on a string, we would never experience the intellectual and spiritual growth he wants us to have and would miss an important part of the abundant life he intends for us.

2. *The need for intimacy with Christ.* Even though it is greatly reassuring to know that Christ guides willing people in spite of their confusion, there is little denying that this confusion can often cause us to feel somewhat distant from him. The more perfectly we understand Christ's leading, the more deeply we will feel a sense of communion with him, a sense of intimacy which can only serve to make us more fruitful in our work for him.

3. *Our need for good mental health.* If we do not use our intellects to discern God's will, we may become vulnerable to unhealthy approaches to guidance which can result in emotional problems. We will look at some of these imbalanced approaches in part III.

4. *The fact that God has commanded it.* We are commanded in Scripture to use our understanding to discern God's will, and this alone should settle the matter. It would be hypocritical to claim on the one hand to be willing to do God's will, but on the other hand not to be willing to follow this clear command of his. It may be said that the person who is being empowered by God's Spirit to want to do his will is going to have a natural

desire to use his or her mind in seeking it.

If we grant, then, that using our minds is important in guidance, we need to go further and say what exactly this means. We will see that our responsibility is actually twofold. First, we should study Scripture, coming to understand as fully as possible the guidance God has already given. Then we have a responsibility to use our reason to make a logical choice about God's will, as opposed to looking for supernatural indications or purely intuitive impressions of his guidance.

Understanding the Role of Scripture

It is beyond my purposes here to go into a lengthy discussion of how to study the Bible. For an excellent treatment of this subject I urge you to read *Knowing Scripture* by R. C. Sproul.[1] My purpose here is simply to consider what role the Bible should play in complex decision making.

In chapter two we noted that complex decisions cannot be fully resolved simply through biblical principles. Thus, I should not expect to find a principle in the Bible which will tell me once and for all to marry Valerie Johnson or to become a biologist. I should, in short, avoid thinking that I will find the final answer to a specific complex decision in the pages of the Bible. And I should see that irrelevant biblical passages should not be expected to reveal God's will to me.

But this does not mean that the Bible should play no role in complex decision making. It has a most significant role. And the person who is serious about doing God's will should be one for whom studying Scripture is a regular and frequent practice. Here we will find Psalm 1:1-3 most instructive:

Blessed is the man who walks not in the counsel of the wicked, nor stands in the way of sinners, nor sits in the seat of scoffers; but his delight is in the law of the LORD, and on his law he meditates day and night. He is like a tree planted by streams of water, that yields its fruit in its season, and its leaf does not wither. In all that he does, he prospers.

In this beautiful passage the psalmist gives a promise to the person who meditates on the law of the Lord; that is, the one who is giving constant and close attention to God's teaching. In referring to the law of the Lord, the psalmist is talking especially about the written teaching of God—the Pentateuch at the time of the writing of the psalm, but today the entire canon of Scripture. The promise he makes is twofold: First, the person who meditates on God's written Word will be *fulfilled* (this is the meaning of the word *blessed* that begins the psalm). Second, this person will be *fruitful.* The psalmist pictures him enjoying a prosperous life, bearing fruit as naturally as a tree that receives abundant nourishment. This is not a suggestion that the Christian will necessarily enjoy material wealth or success in worldly terms; the psalms which follow show again and again that the godly person may experience adversity and will not necessarily enjoy prosperity by the world's standards. But the psalm does assure us of success by God's standards and of a life that will be fruitful for Christ because it is lived in line with his will. The person who meditates on God's Word, in short, will be the one who is empowered to live a life reflective of his will.

The writer of the psalm does not go on to explain precisely how studying Scripture functions to keep us in the will of God; he simply indicates that this will be the case. I believe we can, however, see at least five logical ways in which the Scriptures help us at this point.

Studying Scripture deepens our consciousness of God. This is the most basic and obvious advantage of Bible study. It is a simple fact that most of what goes on in our lives tends to divert our attention from God. We need disciplines in life which turn our attention back to him, for it is impossible to give any serious consideration to his will if our thoughts are not focused on him. Because the Bible is most basically a book about God, it is an invaluable aid in helping us to concentrate on him.

Studying Scripture also brings us into contact with God. When we read with a prayerful spirit there is a sense in which our reading actually brings us closer to God. This does not mean the Bible cannot be read in a purely academic sense. But the fact is that when we approach the Bible we are approaching words which God himself authored through his Holy Spirit; thus as we allow his Spirit to guide us in our study, we are doing more than reading facts—we are allowing ourselves to hear *God speak.* As we allow the Spirit and the Word to work together, our desire for his will often deepens and we find ourselves more capable of understanding his guidance. Our minds and hearts are brought into communion with God in a way that best enables him to speak with us and guide us.

Furthermore, the Scriptures inform us of God's principles. While our complex decisions are not usually resolved through the mechanical application of some biblical principle, there are usually principles which apply to our decisions and should influence them. We must be constantly learning and reviewing the principles of a Christian lifestyle, as there is virtually never a decision we face which does not require some knowledge of biblical norms.

Biblical passages may also confirm a particular decision. On occasion we may find in reading Scripture that we experience a sense of inspiration to do what the passage is talking about, and thereafter the passage serves as a constant encouragement and reminder of this call. St. Paul, for instance, in Romans 15:9-13 quotes several Old Testament verses that apparently profoundly influenced his decision to evangelize the Gentiles. We are not talking here about applying Scripture to irrelevant situations, but about taking a passage in context and being moved by the Spirit to do what it says. A person reading about the great revival that followed Nehemiah's leading the Israelites to rebuild the wall of Jerusalem, for example, might catch a vision for bringing new life to a church through motivating the members to work together on a certain project.

It is important here to stress that guidance in this sense should never be taken from Scripture alone; in all cases, one's inspiration should be carefully checked against other considerations of guidance. A person who is visionary by nature is likely to have a lot more inspirations than could ever be practically carried out. Yet there is no denying that the Holy Spirit will sometimes use a passage of Scripture to give a unique sense of inspiration which will stand the test of other logical considerations. When this happens, one has a special gift from God which thereafter will serve as a confirmation of the call.

Finally, the Bible can be an invaluable aid in praying for guidance. In the psalms we find quite a few prayers for guidance which can be read as our own prayer when seeking God's will. Psalm 143:8, 10 is one of these: "Teach me the way I should go, for to thee I lift up my soul. . . . Teach me to do thy will, for thou art my God! Let thy good spirit lead me on a level path!" There are also prayers for a willing spirit, such as Psalm 51:10-12: "Create in me a clean heart, O God, and put a new and right spirit within me. Cast me not away from thy presence, and take not thy holy Spirit from me. Restore to me the joy of thy salvation, and uphold me with a willing spirit." Other prayers for guidance can be found in Psalms 5:8; 19:12-14; 25:4-5, 21; 27:11; 31:3-4; 86:11; 119:5, 10, 35-36, 80, 133, 176; 141:3-4.

The Nitty-Gritty
The Bible, then, helps us in a variety of ways in our search to know God's will. As John White says:

God does not desire to guide us magically. He wants us to know his mind. He wants us to grasp his very heart. We need minds so soaked with the content of Scripture, so imbued with biblical outlooks and principles, so sensitive to the Holy Spirit's prompting that we will know instinctively the upright step to take in any circumstance, small or great. . . .

Through the study of [Scripture] you may become acquainted with the ways and thoughts of God.[2]

Understanding this, however, is of no use unless we put this knowledge into practice. Each of us needs a time of daily Bible study, in the context of a regular devotional time. Psalm 1 speaks of the importance of meditating upon God's Word day and night, and while this does not mean that every waking thought has to be about Scripture, it does suggest that we should very frequently be thinking about teachings of Scripture and considering their relevance to the situations in which we find ourselves.

From a practical standpoint this is not likely to happen unless we have a daily discipline of Bible reading. The regularity may be far more important than the actual amount of time spent. It is much more valuable to spend ten minutes a day reading the Bible than to spend two hours once a week, for the daily habit will keep the Scriptures in the forefront of our thinking. And I believe that faithfulness in this area gives the Holy Spirit maximum freedom to use the Scriptures in guiding us in God's will.

Often the best approach is to work through the entire Bible, either from front to back or according to a particular daily study program. In addition, it is helpful to read a psalm or two, as the psalms often direct our attention to prayer.

Beyond this it should also be said that in making a major decision we should spend some additional time reading any portions of Scripture that relate directly to that decision. Anyone considering the pastorate, for instance, should become intimately acquainted with the biblical teaching on the role of the pastor and the church. Here the help of a minister or someone else with a thorough knowledge of the Bible is invaluable. Under normal circumstances, however, I believe it is best to study from the standpoint of gaining a greater understanding of the entire Bible, as opposed to studying for a particular decision.

In giving this advice I am, to be sure, speaking from my own experience. Each of us must find what works best for her or him. But in the absence of other ideas, it is often best to begin with what has worked well for others and then to change it as we begin to sense what disciplines are most beneficial to our own growth in Christ.

Thinking
Things
Through

7

WE HAVE STRESSED the importance of Bible study in guidance, but have also shown that we cannot expect the final answer to a complex decision to come from the Bible. From where, then, does the final answer come? In popular thought it is often supposed that one should expect it to come in some direct, supernatural fashion or else through an inward, mystical sense of God's leading. But in this chapter I will stress that the precedence in guidance should really be given to careful, logical decision making. I conclude this from the fact that in the overwhelming majority of decisions noted in the New Testament God's will was discerned through a reasoned decision. Human reason was the channel through which God's will was normally known; discerning his will boiled down to a matter of making a sound, logical choice.

While this can be documented from various places in the New Testament, it comes across most obviously in the example of the apostle Paul. Although Paul is popularly imagined as one who received frequent supernatural guidance, on the whole it seems these instances were few. In the large majority of cases Paul merely followed the dictates of his sanctified reason; that is, reason dedicated to serving God. Two broad examples from Paul's experience should suffice to prove this point.

Choosing a Path

Paul's evangelistic itinerary seems to have been based primarily on logical considerations. Let us look at Romans 15:18-24, where Paul discloses how he determined where he would evangelize:

> For I will not venture to speak of anything except what Christ has wrought through me to win obedience from the Gentiles, by word and deed, by the power of signs and wonders, by the power of the Holy Spirit, so that from Jerusalem and as far round as Illyricum I have fully preached the gospel of Christ, thus making it my ambition to preach the gospel, not where Christ has already been named, lest I build on another man's foundation, but as it is written,
>
> "They shall see who have never been told of him, and
> they shall understand who have never heard of him."
>
> This is the reason why I have so often been hindered from coming to you. But now, since I no longer have any room for work in these regions, and since I have longed for many years to come to you, I hope to see you in passing as I go to Spain, and to be sped on my journey there by you, once I have enjoyed your company for a little.

It is interesting that in this passage Paul does not talk about supernatural guidance in planning his missionary travels. It is apparent, rather, that he made logical decisions about where to go, in light of which areas were most in need of his service. Paramount in his thinking was the strategy of visiting unevangelized territory. He felt he would lay the broadest foundation by doing this, and beginning with this logical assumption he proceeded to determine where to go.

Thus, in 1 Corinthians 16:5-9, where Paul tells the Corinthians he intends to stay at Ephesus until Pentecost, he claims his decision is based on the fact that "a wide door for effective work has opened to me." He makes no claim to extraordinary revelation, as he surely would have done if it were present. He decided to stay in Ephesus simply because the opportunity for fresh evangelizing was present. A logical decision on the basis of circumstantial evidence led Paul to this conclusion about God's will.

In addition to the strategy of visiting unevangelized territory, Paul was also strongly influenced by the desire to revisit his former converts in order to instruct them and fellowship with them. In the letter to the Romans, when Paul tells of his intentions to visit them, he bases this not on any extraordinary sign, but on the fact that he has longed for many years to visit them and that he has run out of fresh territory to evangelize in the east. As a result he boldly declares that it will be God's will for him to visit his Roman friends (15:32) once he has fulfilled the remaining responsibility of delivering a contribution to the poor in Jerusalem (15:25-31).[1] The interplay of logical factors in his decision making is interesting to observe.

In at least one instance in Paul's traveling, his personal concern for former converts overruled his intention of going ahead to fresh territory. He writes in 2 Corinthians 2:12-13: "When I came to Troas to preach the gospel of Christ, a door was opened for me in the Lord; but my mind could not rest because I did not find my brother Titus there. So I took leave of them and went on to Macedonia." John Allan makes some interesting observations on this incident:

> Here we have a striking minor change of plan. Paul had evidently arranged to meet Titus at Troas, and he had every inducement to adhere to that plan because the evangelistic opportunity was great "in the Lord," that is, the favourable circumstances point to the Will of Christ in the matter. Yet Paul went on to Macedonia, simply because his concern for the Corinthian Church tormented him so that

he could not settle to work but hurried, forward on the
route so as to meet Titus and hear his report [on the church]
the sooner. If his letter and Titus's visit had failed, the
Church at Corinth would practically cease to exist as a
Christian force, and he would have to excommunicate them
and hand them over to Satan's realm. His passionate concern for his dear friends and his anxiety for the contin-
uance of the Christian cause in Corinth made it impossible
for him to consider any other service of Christ in the mean-
time. Nothing could show more clearly that Paul was no
fanatic, depending blindly on direct, particular guidance,
and unshakably confident in that guidance.[2]

Regardless of the factor that was prominent in Paul's mind at
the time, his travel decisions in general were based not on
supernatural guidance but on the same sort of logical process
that modern Christians would use. He did not wait for dramatic guidance, but merely looked for the most obvious
and logical opportunity to invest his time and energy for
Christ in the most fruitful way.

Selecting Church Leaders

Paul's appointment of leaders in the early church was also
based primarily on rational considerations. Although Paul
himself received a dramatic call to the ministry, there is no
evidence that he ever required this same experience of others.
When, for instance, he gives instructions about how to choose
church leaders (1 Tim. 3:1-13; Tit. 1:5-9), there is absolutely
no mention of need for a supernatural call. Judgment is to be
based purely on one's ability and the quality of one's faith.
Likewise, where we see Paul choosing leaders himself, there is
no indication he required a specific call.

Kenneth Pike observes two interesting examples of Paul's
using reason in leadership selection. The first example is
of Paul's choice of Silas and Timothy to be his missionary
companions.

From Paul's point of view, why did he choose the two? By

divine orders? ... One finds no evidence of such, but rather sees consecrated judgment in confident action on the basis of the proved character of the two men. Silas had first been chosen by a council as trustworthy, and as one of the "leading men among the brethren" (Acts 15:22); Timothy was "well spoken of by the brethren" (Acts 16:2). These two missionary calls were based on sound judgment, not on feelings.[3]

Regarding Paul's disagreement with Barnabas over the selection of Mark to travel with them, Pike says the following:

The first split of a "mission board" came on the basis of judgment over the fitness of a candidate. Neither Paul nor Barnabas argued that God had directly revealed to him that Mark should or should not go again to the field. The "sharp contention" was on the basis of judgment, since "Paul thought not good to take with them him who withdrew from them from Pamphylia, and went not with them to the work" (Acts 15:38). Judgment, not feeling, as to God's guidance seems to be implied by the words "thought not good."[4]

It appears, then, that Paul regarded rational judgment of a person's qualities as the prime factor constituting a call to Christian leadership. The need for a dramatic supernatural call, such as Paul himself received, was not emphasized. Likewise, our popular notion that a call may come through an inner sense of leading, without outward evidence of ability, finds no support in Paul's teaching.

It appears that in both travel planning and leadership selection Paul made use of his God-given rational faculties in solving most of his decisions. For Paul, discerning God's will was mainly a matter of making sound, logical judgments, in light of what course appeared most glorifying to God. We must conclude that this process of rational discernment should also be our normal approach to discovering God's will.

In addition to Paul's example, we could also note specific places where he exhorts believers to use logical judgment in finding God's will. Colossians 1:9 and Ephesians 5:15-17, when carefully interpreted, yield this sense.[5] But we are in danger of belaboring the point, which is only too obvious by now. It is through our normal, rational decision processes that we discover God's leading, provided that we approach our decision making with a willingness to do God's will. We must agree with the conclusion of James Jauncy, "Guidance is largely consecrated and sanctified thinking."[6] While God can, if he chooses, lead us contrary to reason, we may trust that in such cases he will make his directions unmistakably clear. Apart from such dramatic guidance, our responsibility is to make as sound a decision as possible, trusting that he in his providence will give us all the information we need to decide within his will.

In the final section of this book we will want to consider specifically the question of how we should go about making a logical decision which is glorifying to Christ. We will first, however, find it helpful to take a special look at two areas which when misunderstood can threaten a sound approach to Christian decision making: supernatural guidance and inward guidance.

Improper
Approaches
to Guidance

Visions,
Prophecies
and Fleeces

8

SUPERNATURAL GUIDANCE and inward guidance (guidance through intuition) are two widely misunderstood means of knowing God's will. We have said that God will normally use our sanctified reason to reveal his will to us. Yet occasionally we find dramatic examples of God's guiding someone by more direct means. So we need to examine the place of these experiences in our understanding of how we gain knowledge of God's will.

Supernatural guidance could come in either of two ways: *directly* to me, through a vision, sign, dream, voice, angel and so on; or *indirectly*, through another person's prophecy. In this chapter we will look at both of these areas. In addition, it will be helpful to take a special look at the question of "putting out a fleece," or "fleecing." Although this is really just a form of direct, supernatural guidance (where I ask God for a specific sign), many Christians who make use of the practice would not claim to believe in supernatural guidance. Thus, it will be good to take a separate look at this area.

The Exceptions and the Rules

Many Christians wonder why they should not occasionally receive supernatural guidance. This is a particular problem for new Christians, but I find that older Christians are often troubled by it as well. And some believers actually end up thinking this sort of guidance should be the norm. The problem most often comes from realizing the broad extent to which supernatural guidance occurs in Scripture. If people of faith in the Bible received guidance in a direct manner, and if we are now likewise saints through the work of Christ, then should we not also expect such guidance from God?

Some pastors and teachers will answer yes, you should expect this sort of guidance as a regular experience. The result is often that the believer ends up frustrated with the lack of such experiences, if not deluded with imagined theophanies.

Most pastors and teachers, however, will say that such guidance should not often be expected. The stock reason given is that unlike the saints of the Bible we now possess the full canon of Holy Scripture and are now indwelt by the Holy Spirit. But this answer is really beside the point. The early Christians in the book of Acts had received the Holy Spirit, yet they still received supernatural guidance at times, and the guidance was not a revelation of moral or doctrinal truths, but guidance for complex decisions which could not have been resolved by Scripture alone. Thus, even though they were filled with the Spirit, they still needed occasional direct guidance, and this guidance would have been necessary even if they had possessed the entire New Testament.

But while the stock answer does not deal adequately with the issue, there are substantial reasons why we should not normally expect supernatural guidance. First, when all the instances of guidance are considered, we are struck by the sparsity of such guidance in the early church. It seems that in the great majority of decisions there was no experience of supernatural guidance. This seems true even with the apostle Paul; Acts records less than ten instances of direct guidance received by him, and the evidence is overwhelming that in the bulk of his day-to-day decisions supernatural guidance played no role (see chap. 7).

Further, it is by no means evident that the majority of Christians in the early church ever received supernatural guidance, or for that matter that most of the apostles experienced it after Pentecost. It must be concluded that supernatural guidance was a decidedly exceptional experience in the New Testament church.

Second, there is no statement in the Old or New Testament telling us either to seek or to expect supernatural guidance. If God had wished us to rely on such guidance, he would surely have given us a command to that effect within his Word.

Furthermore, there are several common-sense reasons for not expecting supernatural guidance. For one thing, such direct, dramatic encounters with God could be terribly frightening to us. Martin Luther states, "Our nature cannot bear even a small glimmer of God's direct speaking.... The dreams and visions of the saints are horrifying ... at least after they are understood."[1] The late James H. Miers, former pastor of Fourth Presbyterian Church in Washington, D.C., said that he prayed hard for a supernatural revelation from God. When it finally came, it scared him half to death! Beyond this obvious psychological hazard, we can also see that supernatural guidance could pose severe trials for our faith. We would be inclined to think of ourselves as more spiritual than others. And we would not be motivated to take the sort of personal responsibility for making decisions that really develops faith.

But while we must conclude that we should not normally expect supernatural guidance, it would be unwise to go to the dispensationalist extreme of thinking such guidance *never* occurs in our present age.[2] It seems that there might be certain occasions where direct leading would be necessary. The most probable would be if God would wish to lead us to do something which we would never consider doing on the basis of reason alone.

In the examples of supernatural guidance in Acts, it seems that believers were led to conclusions they would not have reached through normal decision making. In some cases the guidance was repugnant to reason. When Philip was directed by an angel to go to a desert road (Acts 8:26), it was doubtful he would have decided this on his own. Reason would have dictated staying in Samaria where an incredible revival was underway and his services were needed. Likewise, when Paul was struck down on the Damascus road, the guidance given could not possibly have been further from his present intentions. And the vision to venture into Macedonia (Acts 16:9-10) came at a time when he was probably perplexed and lacking logical insight into the next step to take.

In other cases, God's purpose might be to provide an unmistakable point of reference through direct leading which would serve as reassurance in the face of future challenges. Most likely this divine strategy was in mind in the dramatic commissioning of Paul, as Bob Mumford observes:

Paul had the need for a strong point of reference . . . , something he would never forget! God told Ananias in the vision, "For I will show him (Saul) how great things he must suffer for my name's sake." Paul was beaten, jailed, stoned, and left as dead for the sake of the gospel. But God had spoken to him in proportion to the degree of challenge he would face. . . . And he never forgot what happened to him on the road to Damascus.[3]

It is also possible that God would choose to guide supernaturally simply to remind us that he is free to communicate in any way at all and is not bound by any of our preconceptions. But we are certainly not impious in saying that supernatural guidance is something we should not expect or seek in the Christian life. Those who do receive it will probably not experience it often, and most of us will never experience it. We should not think of ourselves as less spiritual because God has not intervened directly in our lives in this way. Supernatural guidance, in fact, could signify spiritual immaturity as much as anything. God might feel compelled to use it to jar someone into the realization that he or she is headed in the wrong direction, but ideally the person should have concluded this without dramatic aid. Of course, all experiences of supernatural guidance do not indicate spiritual immaturity, but neither do they imply spiritual superiority.

The Place of Prophecy

What about the special cases where I receive supernatural guidance indirectly through another person's prophecy? Christians, especially those in charismatic circles, have sometimes been troubled because someone has claimed a revelation of guidance for them which they have never before entertained as God's will. Marriages have been entered into, engagements broken off and vocational decisions resolved, simply because one person claimed a prophecy of God's will for another.

What is the best way to go about evaluating prophecies given to us? I believe the answer is simple: we can disregard them completely. For one thing, there is no instance of a prophecy's being regarded as guidance in the New Testament after Pentecost. Likewise, there is no statement in the New Testament to the effect that we should look on prophecy as a possible source of guidance.[4]

Furthermore, when Paul received prophetic counsel not to go to Jerusalem from friends who predicted disaster, he ignored it (Acts 21:4). There is no indication in Acts that Paul disobeyed God's will; instead the impression is given that he followed God's will by proceeding to Jerusalem. While he recognized the validity of his friends' prediction of doom (Acts 20:22-23),[5] he did not believe that the counsel stemming from their prophecy was divine. Thus, it seems that their counsel was a human conclusion resulting from their expe-

rience of revelation but not received as a direct part of it. F.
F. Bruce's observation here is pertinent: "It was natural that
his friends who by the prophetic spirit were able to foretell
his tribulation and imprisonment should try to dissuade him
from going on."[6]

We are not denying, then, that prophecy can at times function as prediction.[7] But we are insisting that it never has to be
taken as guidance. There is just no clear New Testament mandate to this effect. We must agree with Michael Harper:

Prophecies which tell other people what they are to do—are
to be regarded with great suspicion. "Guidance" is never
indicated as one of the uses of prophecy. Paul was told what
would happen to him if he went to Jerusalem, but was not
told either to go or refrain from going. His friends may
have advised him concerning this—but the guidance did
not come from the prophecy. Agabus foretold a famine, but
his prophecy gave no instructions as to what should be done
about it. On the whole in the New Testament guidance is
given direct to the individual—not through another person
—as was common in the Old Testament. For instance, although Cornelius was told by an angel to send for Peter
(Acts 10:5), Peter himself was told to go with them through
an independent agency (Acts 10:20). There may be excep-
tions to this—but if so they are very rare. This gift is not intended to take the place of common sense or the wisdom
which comes from God and which manifests itself through
our natural faculties.[8]

This is not to imply that the counsel of others is not very important, and we will argue in chapter thirteen that counsel is
vital in making major decisions. But we may be freed forever
from the fear that someone's counsel would necessarily have
to be taken as God's will simply because that person claimed a
prophetic revelation. I may assume that in all cases if the
prophecy is genuine guidance, God will make this abundantly
evident to me through more direct means. Apart from such
direct evidence, I may feel free to disregard the counsel based

on a prophetic utterance as an unfortunate misjudgment on the part of the one offering it.

Putting Out a Fleece

The practice of putting out a fleece is often recommended as a method of guidance. Because of its popularity, we need to take a careful look at it.

In Judges 6 an Israelite named Gideon is asked by God to take a very small army and attack the neighboring Mideonites. Gideon finds the command so incredible that he asks God for a special sign as evidence: Gideon will put a lamb's fleece on the ground, and if God has indeed spoken, then in the morning the fleece will be wet and the ground around it dry. God responds as Gideon requested. The next night, just to be sure, Gideon once again asks for a sign from God: this time to make the fleece dry and the ground wet. God again responds according to Gideon's request.

From this incident comes our practice of "fleecing." When faced with a decision, we ask God to provide a particular sign as proof of his will. There is a good deal of Old Testament precedence for this practice beyond the Gideon passage. The practice of casting lots to find God's will, for instance, was extremely common among the Israelites (see Prov. 16:33). The Mosaic Law, in fact, prescribed that priests fulfill this function for persons wishing to inquire of the Lord (Deut. 33:8). This practice was still common among the Jews in New Testament days; thus through the casting of lots Zechariah was assigned to temple duty (Lk. 1:9), and the early believers chose a successor for Judas (Acts 1:15-26).

But it is most important to note that after the day of Pentecost there is no biblical example of casting lots or anything akin to putting out a fleece. It seems that after this time the practice was no longer necessary. I think we should conclude that the Spirit-filled believer has all the inner resources necessary for decision making. For Christians, fleecing should really be seen as an abdication of personal responsibility.

This is important to emphasize, for in this area we tend to fall into foolish practices. A friend of mine, for instance, asked God one morning to show him whether or not he should attend class by making the stoplight ahead either red or green! I realize that fleecing is often approached with considerably more care and maturity. But in most cases it amounts to an attempt to oversimplify our decisions.

There is only one approach to this practice which, under certain conditions, I would think appropriate. This approach I would not technically term *fleecing*. In fleecing, God is usually asked for a sign which has no particular relevance to the issues in a decision (the stoplight, for instance). This kind of practice should always be avoided. But occasionally there is value in asking God to show his will by making certain details *which are directly relevant to a decision* work out in a certain way. This might be advisable if one arrives at a true impasse.

A friend, for instance, was seeking God's will regarding the purchase of a particular home. After a careful analysis of the situation, he made an offer to the owner of the house. When after some time he had not received a reply, he prayed that the owner would give him a positive response by 5 P.M. the next day if God wished him to purchase the home. Otherwise, he would feel free before God to begin looking elsewhere. The owner did indeed phone him, shortly before 5 P.M., accepting the offer, and since all other signals were positive, he took this as a remarkable confirmation of God's will.

In this case my friend made a mature and responsible request for a sign from God. He had done his homework, carefully analyzed the situation, and done what he could to get the final piece of information he needed—the owner's selling price. Now his hands were tied, and since he knew it would be irresponsible to wait indefinitely for a reply, he asked God for special guidance. But he did not ask God for some irrelevant sign, but merely that the circumstances of his transaction would work out in a specific, positive way. Being at an impasse, he was quite justified in praying as he did.

All of us can expect occasionally to confront similar circumstances, where we face a genuine roadblock to making a decision we otherwise feel God would have us make. In such a case we would be justified in asking God to remove this roadblock as a specific indication of his will. We must simply be careful not to use this sort of request to avoid responsibility for careful thinking. Only when we face a real obstacle would this approach be recommended. And then it would be best to think of it not as putting out a fleece but rather as asking God for some explicit circumstantial guidance.

Under no circumstances should we ask for a sign which is not directly pertinent to the details of our decision. Regardless of the impasse we might be up against, such an approach to decision making is injudicious and often outright superstitious.

Looking
for an
Inward Sign

9

OFTENTIMES RATHER THAN LOOKING for an outward sign,
Christians will seek an intuitive impression of the Holy Spirit's
leading—a hunch, an inspiration, a "warm feeling" that something is God's will. This is distinguished from supernatural
guidance in that there is no audible voice or visible sign, but
simply a *feeling* about God's leading. Likewise, this is different
from rational thinking in that a conclusion is not reached
from logical argument, but from intuition.

It is popularly assumed that intuition is in some sense the
direct voice of the Holy Spirit. A strong inspiration to do
something is as clear a leading of the Holy Spirit as the audible
voice of God. When someone says, "God spoke to me," most
often he or she means not that God's audible voice was heard
but that a sense of inspiration to move in a certain direction
was felt. Many people refer to this as, "the still small voice."[1]

This inward guidance is understood as having two facets.
On the one hand, God's leading will be known by strong, posi-

tive feelings to go in a certain direction. Apart from the experience of such feelings, some say, it is wrong to proceed. On the other hand, negative feelings, or "pangs of conscience," about a certain action are considered a direct command from God not to go ahead. "When in doubt, don't," as the popular expression goes.

What is common to both these aspects of inward guidance is the belief that God speaks *directly* through our feelings; that is, that our intuition is the voice of his Spirit. When we come to the question of whether there is truth to this assumption, we have to be cautious in our reply. I would not want to say that God never speaks through our intuition or that he never influences our feelings in order to tell us something. To say this would be severely restrictive of God's providence, and the experiences of numerous Christians suggest otherwise. But there is no question in my mind that many Christians today put an unhealthy emphasis on inward guidance.

There is a tendency to look on intuition as an infallible channel of God's speaking. To question intuition is to question God himself. This understanding reached its height in the Quaker doctrine of the "inner light," which, especially among George Fox and some of the early Quakers, was taken to extremes. Among them the possibility of human error in knowing God's will through intuition was simply not entertained. But even among modern Christians we often find this tendency to regard intuition as a foolproof channel of guidance.

What the Bible Says
When we turn to Scripture, we find no evidence supporting this extreme notion of intuition. I can find no examples in either the Old or New Testament where it is clear that someone discerned God's will through inward guidance. This may seem surprising, but I would challenge the reader to find such an instance. You might think of places in Acts where reference is made to the Holy Spirit's guiding someone to do something; but a careful analysis of each passage leads to the con-

clusion that the reference is more likely either to direct supernatural guidance or to a rational decision.[2]

There is also no clear statement in the Old or New Testament telling us that we should attempt to discern God's will
merely through intuition. There are several verses which are
popularly used to support inward guidance as the prime
means of knowing God's will, but when examined in context
they are found not to be dealing with the notion at all.

Colossians 3:15 states: "Let the peace of Christ rule in your
hearts." This is the most popular verse sighted in favor of inward guidance. The Greek word for *rule* means "act as umpire," and it is claimed that Paul is saying we should let peace-
ful feelings umpire our decision making. Examined in context, however, it is plain that this verse is not referring to a personal, subjective feeling of peace, but rather to the corporate
reality of peace which should exist among believers. The verse
does not relate to personal decision making.

Another largely misunderstood verse is 1 John 4:1: "Be-
loved, do not believe every spirit, but test the spirits to see
whether they are of God." It is widely held that the testing of
spirits in this verse refers to judging personal feelings as to
whether they are divinely produced or not. In context, however, the reference is to judging the doctrinal teachings of
teachers who call themselves Christian.

A more complex passage is Romans 14:22-23: "The faith
that you have, keep between yourself and God; happy is he
who has no reason to judge himself for what he approves. But
he who doubts is condemned, if he eats, because he does not
act from faith; for whatever does not proceed from faith is
sin." It is commonly believed that Paul is saying here that we
should take no action whenever we have any reservations. It
must be noted, however, that in this passage he is talking
about those gray areas of morality for which the early Christians had no explicit commandment, such as drinking, eating
meat or observing certain holidays. In these areas, Paul says,
let your conscience be your guide: if in doubt, then don't.[3]

Paul's statements in Romans 14 were not meant for application to broader, more complex decisions; he is simply not dealing with that subject here.

But what about the rest of the Bible? Other biblical passages could be cited which, on a cursory reading, might seem to be talking about seeking God's will purely through intuition, but on closer analysis are found not to be dealing with this at all. We must conclude that there is no biblical basis for the notion that intuition should be regarded as an infallible indication of the Holy Spirit's leading, akin to hearing the audible voice of God.

This is not to suggest that God never leads Christians through their feelings. But we must see that for most of us our feelings are so diverse and so changeable that it would be unreasonable to expect them to be the sole barometer of God's will. In any case, if we suspect God is trying to convey a special message to us through our intuition, we have the right (and really the responsibility) to check this out through other means. Oliver Barclay says that "such guidance must be checked by more objective standards, and it would seem to be our duty to pray that God will rather give us *reasons* for such actions."[4] Taking precautions with intuition should not be thought of as a lack of faith, but as our responsibility to guard against error.

Mirror of Our Minds

We have been discussing the role of intuition as a spiritual phenomenon. But it must also be seen as a *psychological* event. Intuition in many cases is revealing something about myself: it is often a glimpse of my deepest feelings; in short, it tells me what underneath I really want to do. Intuition gives me crucial insight into my subconscious, the seat of my feelings. From this angle intuition can be seen as having a most important function in guidance. My deepest desires are often significant in finding God's will. They tell me something about how God has made me and thus about the kind of responsibilities he might want me to assume.

We will not, to be sure, conclude that any desire is ever an infallible sign of God's will. It is merely one factor to be considered along with others. Even my deepest-seated feelings can change; and even where they are consistent, they may or may not be significant in relation to God's will.

Furthermore, while intuition is an important indication of my feelings, it is not an infallible gauge of them. And most importantly, it is not an indication of how I might feel if I had further information. When intuition speaks, my subconscious has processed information more quickly than my conscious mind, and my intuition is telling me what my subconscious has concluded. But this means that my intuition will only be as good as the information to which I have been exposed. Thus, I must be careful about taking intuition too seriously.

In the chapter on desires we will look more closely at the matter of understanding our feelings in light of God's will. For now, let us merely say that feelings are important in knowing God's will, but they are not the infallible voice of God. When I feel a strong sense of intuition, rather than say, "God has spoken to me," I would better say, "My subconscious has spoken, and this may indicate what God is saying."

Making
Decisions

IV

Beginning to Decide: Considering Personal Desires

10

HAVING DISCUSSED the roles and limitations of supernatural guidance and inward guidance, we will now want to turn to the subject of making a logical decision. We have established the importance of sound, reasoned thinking in discerning God's will. But we are still left with a major question: Just how should we go about making a Christ-honoring, logical decision?

This is a vital question, for I find that while many Christians realize that discerning God's will boils down to making a rational decision, tremendous confusion exists over how to weigh the various factors involved. In the remaining chapters we will look at the process of decision making more closely.

I admit that I approach this section with certain reservations, for I do not want to imply that there is an easy answer to our complicated decisions. Our decision making as believers, at least in major areas, must always be a somewhat difficult process, and we have to be leery of oversimplified approaches and pat formulas. At the same time, I believe that we often make it more complicated than necessary. There are certain principles which can generally simplify our understanding of God's will.

First Steps in Decision Making

Certain distinctions will be made here which will be basic to our discussion. To begin with, it will be helpful to classify the factors in a logical decision under four basic areas:

Desire: my personal feelings about a particular alternative

Ability: my competence for handling the responsibilities of a particular alternative

Circumstances: opportunities available to me (open doors, closed doors)

Counsel: the opinions of other people about my decision

This fourfold classification should include every factor we might consider in a complex decision. Our problems in discerning God's will (beyond attitude problems) almost always result from difficulty in understanding the role that one of these factors should play. We will take a close look at each of these factors: how they interrelate, and how they should be allowed to influence our understanding of God's will.

It will also be helpful to distinguish between *major* and *minor decisions.* In drawing this distinction, we will employ a word whose original sense has practically vanished from our popular vocabulary: the term *vocation.* We use this word today to refer to a person's profession. But during the Protestant Reformation the term was used by the Reformers in a much broader sense to refer to any major area of a person's life. Not only was a person's profession a vocation, but also his or her family, citizenship, church affiliation, community involvement, hobbies and so on.

We will make use of this term to distinguish between major and minor decisions. By a major decision, we will mean a decision *for a vocation,* that is, a decision to enter a major area of commitment. A minor decision will be one made *within a vocation,* that is, to fulfill the responsibilities of the commitment.

A decision to marry, to have children, to choose a certain profession or job or to attend a certain college would be a major decision. A minor decision, on the other hand, would be one to carry out the commitment already made to the vocation; for example, the decision to take a vacation with the family, to make a certain business deal, to take a certain course at school.

While this distinction may seem simplistic, we will find it quite helpful in understanding how various factors should relate in our decision making. It will be particularly helpful in understanding the roles of personal desires and circumstances in knowing God's will.

How Desires Fit In

No one area creates more confusion in knowing God's will than the role of personal wishes. Does doing God's will mean my desires should be affirmed, or denied?

Many people simply assume that personal desire is the all-important sign of God's will. "Love God and do what you wish," as the popular expression goes. But this assumes that if we love God our wishes will automatically conform to his will. In fact, because we are sinners, this will not always be the case. The Bible confirms that Christians will have to choose undesirable alternatives at times.

On the other hand, I find that some Christians go to the opposite extreme and believe that a Spirit-led decision will always lead to suffering. They think that God's will and their wishes will never coincide. But such thinking is every bit as distorted as the notion of loving God and doing what you wish, for it ignores the biblical evidence that God sometimes creates desires within us in order to guide us. In both cases an important biblical truth is carried to an unhealthy extreme.

What is really needed is an understanding of the truth on *both* sides of this coin. There is a strong sense in which self-denial must operate in our decisions as Christians, but there is also a sense in which our desires must be affirmed in order to recognize God's will. A mature Christian perspective demands that we see the relationship between self-denial and self-affirmation and try to strike a balance between the two.

On the positive side, the biblical doctrine of providence suggests that God works within the redeemed believer to form desires which accord with his will. Consider Paul's familiar statement in Philippians 2:12-13: "work out your own salvation with fear and trembling; for God is at work in you, both to will and to work for his good pleasure." Here Paul implies that God is working within us to create certain feelings. This is clear from Paul's use of the word *work,* which in the Greek is *energeō,* from which we get our term *energy.* When Paul says, "God is at work in you," he is saying that God is *energizing* you in the direction of his will. God is giving you the creative inspiration you need to make decisions which agree with his will. He is providentially forming in you certain desires which will move you in the direction he wants you to go.

We have already pointed out that Paul's missionary itineraries were strongly influenced by the desire to spend time with former converts (see pp. 63-64). When the urge to be with his friends got too strong, Paul assumed that God was leading him to spend time with them.

Likewise, in his teachings Paul implies that desire is a key sign of God's will in two important decisions—marriage and church vocation. Regarding marriage, Paul indicates that one recognizes God's will for whether or not one should marry through a desire for sexual fulfillment (1 Cor. 7:1-9). We must conclude that desire is a vital factor in the choice of whether to marry and whom to marry. Marrying someone out of sympathy or out of a sense of duty is not to follow God's will. Not that desire is the only factor to consider—there must be compatibility on a variety of plains. But if the desire is not there, no amount of compatibility in other areas will make up for it.

Regarding church vocation, Paul gives the qualifications

for church leadership in 1 Timothy 3, and he begins the section by saying, "If any one aspires to the office of bishop, he desires a noble task" (v. 1). Notice the words *aspires* and *desires* in this verse. Paul assumes that the person who takes on the role of spiritual leadership should have a significant desire to be in that position—that person should have a sense of aspiration toward it.

Paul, in the way he treats these two decisions, is certainly indicating that our desires are an important factor in major decisions. All in all, we must conclude that God exercises his providence in creating our personalities. I may trust that he has not allowed my particular personality to develop by accident but has fashioned my inclinations and preferences as a means of motivating me in certain directions. By looking to the desires that are most basic to my personality, I can gain vital insights into where God is leading me.

But if this is true, where does the responsibility for self-denial come in? We must begin by stressing that *willingness* to deny our desires must always be present if we hope to know and do God's will. While God will not necessarily call me to self-denial in a given decision, I must always be willing to respond if he does. There will be times when circumstances force me to accept an alternative I little desire. Or God could reveal supernaturally that I should go in a direction I would never choose on the basis of personal preference. I must determine in advance that I will follow if God should so lead.

But apart from such direct leading, and whenever circumstances allow freedom of choice, I believe there is a good rule of thumb to follow. Generally speaking, a major decision should be based on personal desire as much as possible. A decision for a particular vocation, in other words, should be based on desire. But decisions made within the vocation (in order to fulfill its responsibilities) may often involve sacrifice and considerable self-denial.

Let me explain. Under most conditions we tend to do our

best work when it is a reflection of what we most want to do. The person who really enjoys being a security guard, for instance, will do a better job than the person who dislikes the role. The man who loves being with his wife and family will be a better husband and father than the one who spends time with them out of a sense of duty. I should conclude, then, that I will do my best work for Christ when I am doing what I most enjoy. I will be able to invest my total personality, and I will be most helpful to other people, since others tend to relate to me best when they sense I am enjoying what I am doing.

Since a decision for a vocation means a long-range commitment of time and energy, it only makes sense that the decision should be based on desire when possible. Without a basic desire to be in the vocation, I will lack the creative energy to carry it out fruitfully.

On the other hand, once I have entered a vocation, my desires will often have to be sacrificed in order to fulfill its short-range responsibilities. By committing myself to a vocation I have pledged myself to a long-range desire: that of successfully meeting the goals of the vocation. In order to satisfy that long-range desire, I will often have to forsake short-range desires which conflict with it.

For example, the men and women who choose the medical profession should be very sure they will enjoy medical work. If they do not experience a basic fulfillment through this vocation, they will lack the momentum to carry out the intensive responsibilities of the work. They will, however, constantly have to sacrifice otherwise worthwhile desires to fulfill the daily demands of the job. While a physician might desire strongly to spend Saturday evening with a church group, for instance, an emergency operation should leave him or her little question as to where the will of God lies, in spite of the intrusion this would be on a well-deserved time of fellowship.

In light of what we are saying, then, it should be clear that the more permanent or time-consuming a vocation, the greater should be our certainty that we really want to be in it.

With respect to the most permanent vocation of all, the vocation of marriage, the highest degree of certainty should be demanded. A couple seeking God's will for marriage should look closely at their desire to spend their lives together. This desire must be strong before they begin to consider the possibility of God's leading them toward marriage.

By the same token, the shorter the commitment involved in a vocation, the greater the freedom we may feel to experiment.

We should see our desires as reflective of how God has made us and as key indicators of the type of responsibilities he would have us assume. We should see it as bad stewardship not to make a careful assessment of our desires. Only someone with a martyr complex would go into an unappealing vocation just because he or she thinks it would be unenjoyable. We may trust that as we choose a vocation that best matches our deepest desires, God will provide abundant opportunity to practice self-denial through the responsibilities of the vocation.

Know Your Needs

At this point we are still left with a major question: How do we really know what our deepest desires are? All of us experience a myriad of desires, from fleeting urges to monumental passions. How are we to sort out from all of these which ones are most significant in knowing God's will?

To begin with, no desire which contradicts Scripture should be heeded. This should go without saying. But beyond this, these are some practical steps which I believe will improve our understanding of what are our most significant desires. I recommend the following five steps when making a major decision:

1. Look for a broad level of desire. Not only should desire for personal fulfillment be present, but there should also be a genuine urge to see other people helped through the vocation. We are happiest when we are helping others. But we are of limited value to others unless we also feel creatively fulfilled through what we are doing. So in most cases, both the desire for creative fulfillment and the desire to help others should be present when choosing a vocation. In addition, there should be a desire for personal growth through the challenges of the vocation. In other words, I should desire the personal qualities which the vocation will produce in me. If I am considering a vocation in music, for instance, I should desire not only to perform, but also to become as proficient in my area as possible.

2. *Experiment!* Basically all thinking about a vocation is speculation until you actually become involved in it. So whenever possible, get involved with a vocation before making a long-range commitment to it. In some cases you may discover that what you thought would be abhorrent work is actually very fulfilling. This has been the case with many missionaries, for instance. Or you might discover just the opposite. I would especially encourage young Christians who are free to do so to experiment with areas of service which might not seem naturally attractive but where the human need is great. There are many short-term missionary projects in America and abroad, for instance, which provide opportunities to do just this.

3. *Look to intuition.* As we stressed in our chapter on inward guidance, our intuition may often be a signal of what we are most deeply feeling.

4. *Put desires to a time test.* If at all possible, avoid choosing a vocation until you have experienced a significant desire toward it for a reasonable period of time. The greater the commitment involved in the vocation, the longer should be the time allowed for your desires to "season." Needless to say, this speaks of the importance of a reasonable engagement period before marriage.

5. *Ask yourself: "How would I advise someone else faced with the same facts?"* Your answer to this question may well give insight into your deepest feelings.

These five steps, I believe, should provide a most helpful basis for evaluating personal feelings. You must remember, though, that regardless of how well you understand your personal desires, you should never see them as an infallible source of guidance. While they are a vital factor to consider, they will not tell you God's will beyond question. Even an obviously God-honoring desire should not be taken uncritically as his leading. Remember that King David of Israel greatly desired to build a temple for God, but God replied that while this was a noble offer, it was simply not in his present timetable for it to be built (1 Kings 8:17-19; 2 Chron. 6:8-9).

Ultimately, you should take your desires seriously only when they have been carefully considered along with the other factors of ability, circumstances and counsel. We move on now to look at these other areas.

Evaluating
Abilities
11

IN ADDITION TO DESIRE, we should also have evidence of personal ability (actual skills or potentials) before choosing a vocation. This would only seem logical. But a surprising number of Christians actually challenge this assumption. Many feel that God's calling to a vocation comes irrespective of personal qualifications. They feel that walking in faith means moving ahead in spite of a lack of ability, trusting God to provide the necessary skills when they are needed and not before.

As a result many Christians enter vocations without carefully assessing their skills and potential for future development. This is quite typical in the area of marriage. So many Christians enter marriage simply "in faith," without seriously considering whether they are capable of living with one another. Likewise, it is common for Christians to enter professions, especially in the area of Christian ministry, without really considering their competence for the work they will face. They trust that God will give them the skills they need once they are in the work, even though they might have shown no previous potential in the area.

But this kind of thinking has little basis in Scripture. More often than not it is based on a faulty understanding of spiritual gifts. The Bible records that God sometimes manifests his power by enabling people to perform in ways in which they previously showed no aptitude. From this it is concluded that God can be expected to lead us into major areas of commitment before we have reasonable assurance of our potential in the area. This is an unfortunate misunderstanding of biblical teaching. In order to correct this common misconception, we will now take a look at the nature and purpose of spiritual gifts in biblical teaching, and then consider the relevance of gifts and abilities to guidance.

Spiritual Gifts

It is considerably beyond my purposes to present an exhaustive study of spiritual gifts. Others are much more qualified for that task. (In particular I would recommend *Fire in the Fireplace* by Charles Hummel.[1]) Here we will simply note some basic facts about spiritual gifts that are pertinent to understanding their role in guidance.

Although teaching on spiritual gifts permeates the entire New Testament, the most extensive passages dealing with the subject are Romans 12:3-8, 1 Corinthians 12—14 and Ephesians 4:7-14, all Pauline writings. If the reader is not familiar with these passages, I recommend reading them as a background to the discussion which follows.

In light of Paul's teaching in these passages, we should note five facts about spiritual gifts:

1. Spiritual gifts are given to every believer. Paul is about as explicit about this as he can be in his discussion in 1 Corinthians 12. "To each is given the manifestation of the Spirit for the common good," he says in verse 7, and throughout the passage it is clear that "the manifestation of the Spirit" refers to spiritual gifts. There is no room in Paul's thinking for the notion that these gifts are the special possession of the ordained clergy; spiritual gifts are given to each member of Christ's body and have no direct relation to a person's official status within the ecclesiastical structure. Each of us must begin with the assumption that he or she is a recipient of this endowment.

2. Spiritual gifts should be understood as a present reality and not merely a phenomenon of the first-century church. Although some within the dispensational camp of theology would claim that the gifts ceased with the formulation of the full canon of Scripture, there is no direct statement to this effect in the Bible, and certainly the evidence in the contemporary church would point to the contrary. Here we must agree with Charles Hummel:

> The New Testament nowhere teaches that these spiritual gifts would be withdrawn. Paul devotes three chapters of his first letter to the Corinthians to the nature, purpose and use of spiritual gifts. Here, if anywhere, one would expect him to identify any temporary gifts and prepare the believers for their phasing out. On the contrary, he not only emphasizes the importance of each charism, but also takes pains to instruct this new Christian community in the proper use of prophecy and tongues in public worship.[2]

3. Spiritual gifts should properly be understood not as human abilities but as special manifestations of the Holy Spirit. A great deal of confusion exists among Christians regarding the exact nature of a spiritual gift. And this confusion is understandable in light of the diversity of gifts which Paul lists in the various passages. Some, such as the gift of administration or the gift of teaching, would appear simply to be the Spirit's use of one's natural ability, leading many to conclude that a spiritual gift is merely an intensification by the Spirit of an innate ability. But on the other hand, there are those gifts which are clearly miraculous in nature (such as faith, tongues, healing) leading many to conclude that a spiritual gift has no real relation to a person's natural talents.

But if Paul's complete teaching on gifts is considered, we

must conclude that the truth lies in neither of these extremes. Paul "makes no distinction between what we call supernatural and natural, spectacular and ordinary, logical and emotional."[3] Paul is concerned not with *what* personal channel the Holy Spirit used, but rather *that* the Holy Spirit worked in a special way. In 1 Corinthians 12:7 Paul describes the spiritual gift as a "manifestation of the Spirit," and this is really his conception of a gift—nothing more, nothing less. The spiritual gift is a special working of God's Spirit through the believer which employs her or his innate ability and personality but is not limited by any of these personal characteristics and often transcends them. Here again Hummel makes a helpful comment:

> A charism is neither a natural ability nor a new impartation which a person *possesses*, but a new functioning of what God has already given, activated and exercised by the power of the Spirit. Arnold Bittlinger defines a charism as a "gracious manifestation of the Holy Spirit, working in and through but going beyond, the believer's natural ability for the common good of the people of God." The charism is a gift because that ability has a new function and power. In its exercise the unity of the divine and the human should be recognized.[4]

4. Spiritual gifts are given specifically for building up the body of Christ. Personal edification, while inevitably a result, is not the primary reason God bestows spiritual gifts. If we look at the specific gifts listed by Paul in various passages, we see in every case, either from the obvious nature of the gift or from the context in which it is presented, that its purpose is to contribute to the edification of Christ's body in a special way. This occurs either through directly contributing to the well-being of other Christians (most of the gifts clearly do this) or through bringing nonbelievers into the fold (the gift of evangelism, especially). In every case the spiritual gift strengthens the body of Christ.

Thus we can see the criterion by which we are to judge

whether we have a spiritual gift: if some service I am performing is helping other Christians in a significant way or bringing others to Christ, then it is quite likely I am making use of a spiritual gift. It should not be supposed, however, that the spiritual gift by definition must be exercised within the context of the Christian community. While the person teaching a Bible class at church may be making obvious use of a spiritual gift, it is also possible that the one teaching English at a public school is using a spiritual gift as well, if through that teaching people are being drawn to Christ. Ultimately the test of a spiritual gift is not the activity itself nor the location where it is exercised, but its effect—is it making a significant contribution to the body of Christ?

5. *A believer may have more than one spiritual gift.* There is an unfortunate assumption among many Christians that each believer has only one gift. Thus it happens that I decide what "my gift" is and then close myself off to the possibility of ministry in other areas. "Why, my gift is teaching, so I really can't consider helping with the hunger mission." But such a perspective is a narrow understanding of Paul's teaching. In two places (1 Cor. 12:31 and 14:1) Paul tells his readers to desire the *gifts* (plural).

In addition, Paul himself demonstrated more than one of the gifts he talks about. He laid claim to both the gift of apostleship (1 Cor. 1:1) and the gift of tongues (1 Cor. 14:18); and he certainly demonstrated contributions to the church of his day in numerous areas which align with spiritual gifts, such as administration, giving, exhortation and teaching. Paul was open to ministering to people on a wide variety of fronts, and this openness is probably best described by his statement, "I have become all things to all men, that I might by all means save some" (1 Cor. 9:22). Paul saw his work not as narrowly dictated by one particular gift but as a need-centered ministry, where he was willing to involve himself in many different sorts of activity in order to advance the gospel and build others up in Christ. Certainly this indicates that Paul left himself open to the possibility that new gifts would be given to him when needs arose.

Spiritual gifts are given, as we have said, to meet needs in the body of Christ. With this purpose in view, it is only logical that one may experience a variety of gifts throughout a lifetime. Each of us must stay open to the possibility of experiencing new gifts for new needs.

The question arises, then, of when it is right to expect Christ to give a gift for a particular ministry and when expecting this is presumptuous. This brings us back to the question of guidance.

Gifts, Abilities and Guidance

Spiritual gifts are special manifestations of the Spirit given to each believer for the sake of the body of Christ. But how does this relate to guidance? Must I have clear evidence of a spiritual gift before I assume God would want me to take on service where such a gift would be needed? Or should I in faith take on certain responsibilities even though to this point I have had no clear evidence of God's desire to gift me in that area?

Here we have to see the answer as depending on the dimension of the commitment involved. In the case of more limited, short-range commitments, we should be willing to experiment with areas of service where we are not certain of our qualifications. Ultimately the only way I can discover whether God wishes to gift me in a certain area or not is to experiment. As I try out an area of service, I discover through the results and through the confirmation of others in the body whether I truly do have a gift in the area. There is no other way of finding out apart from this. If I am interested in finding out about my gifts, it is essential that I have regular involvement in a Christian community, where I can receive feedback from others as I endeavor to meet the needs in the fellowship.

In this context the most important question becomes not, "What is my gift?" but rather, "How can I be of service?" My thinking should not begin with myself but with the needs of others in the body.[5] I may find that there are significant needs which demand gifts I do not have. In such cases it may be well to experiment in this new area to see if the Lord might give me a fruitful ministry in it. The results will often be surprising. Countless Christians have discovered a gift for teaching through responding reluctantly to a need within the fellowship, even though underneath they thought that teaching would be the last way the Spirit would manifest himself through them.

Experimenting is necessary in areas of Christian service where the commitment is limited, and we have the freedom without embarrassment to withdraw if we sense we are not being fruitful. But the greater a commitment of time and service becomes, the lesser should be the sense of freedom to experiment, and the greater should be our advance assurance that we already possess the potential for the work.

Here we should note the advice of Paul in Romans 12:3, where he introduces his discussion of spiritual gifts: "For by the grace given to me I bid every one among you not to think of himself more highly than he ought to think, but to think with sober judgment, each according to the measure of faith which God has assigned him." In the context of the passage, "the measure of faith" refers to the manifestation of the Spirit which one has experienced, that is, the evidence of spiritual gifts. Paul then proceeds in the next several verses to exhort his readers to use their particular gifts. It is interesting that in verse 3 Paul precedes the exhortation not by telling the readers to take bold ventures of faith into areas where they are not certain of their capacities, but to think soberly about how they will serve one another in light of the gifts they already have. Paul is not ruling out the need for experimentation with interests in order to find out what one's gifts are, but his statement indicates that there is a point at which sober thinking must take over and one must avoid venturing into areas where aptitude has not already been evidenced.

Paul does not, to be sure, get technical about just where this point is reached. But we must conclude that the point is unquestionably reached in major vocational decisions. We can see this, for instance, in the advice Paul gives Timothy about choosing church leaders in 1 Timothy 3:

Now a bishop must be above reproach, the husband of one wife, temperate, sensible, dignified, hospitable, an apt teacher, no drunkard, not violent but gentle, not quarrelsome, and no lover of money. He must manage his own household well, keeping his children submissive and respectful in every way; for if a man does not know how to manage his own household, how can he care for God's church? He must not be a recent convert, or he may be puffed up with conceit and fall into the condemnation of the devil; moreover he must be well thought of by outsiders, or he may fall into reproach and the snare of the devil. (vv. 2-7)[6]

Here we see Paul giving a very specific list of qualifications which must be met *in advance* before a particular person would be called into service. There was a similar list of qualifications for deacons (vv. 8-13). Paul does not suggest that a person should be put in a leadership position simply as an experiment to see if he or she might acquire the gifts. He says the qualifications must be in evidence *before* the appointment is made.

Paul notably does not make a fine distinction between spiritual gifts and natural endowments in this passage. He simply mentions *qualifications* which must be met. Paul seems more concerned with character traits than with talent (although talent is definitely important: one must be an "apt teacher" and able to administer). What the list really shows is that in assessing God's call to a vocation of church leadership people are to take everything they know about their personality and potential into account. Not to do this is to act presumptuously. And it is not too great an inference, I believe, to say that this is true with respect to any vocation we would consider as believers.

Thus in the numerous instances in Scripture where God calls a person into a major area of service, while there are cases of further gifts being given after the call, we see few clear examples where the person did not possess at least some basic qualifications for the call before receiving it. One might cite Moses as an exception, since at first he resisted God's call to deliver Israel due to his lack of articulateness. But it should not be overlooked that Moses grew up in Pharaoh's court and was son-in-law of the priest of Midian, two circumstances which uniquely prepared him for the unusual mission into which God called him. And when we look through the Old Testament we find numerous examples where personal abilities clearly preceded God's call to a particular responsibility.[7]

In the New Testament the prime example is Paul. While Paul received special gifts after conversion, the fact remains that he had numerous qualifications before conversion that uniquely suited him for apostleship. He was by nature a person of unusual energy and vision, and his background included considerable administrative experience, a faculty for public speaking, and theological training under one of the most respected Jewish scholars of the day. Thus, while his call to apostleship required a profound reorientation of his mind and heart, it did not by any means plunge him into an area of work incompatible with his personality.

The Scriptures do not give basis to the popular notion that God's call to a vocation is unrelated to our personal qualifications. We should evaluate our gifts, abilities and personality to see whether we have the qualifications needed for a particular vocation. We should not look at this evaluation as a lack of faith, but rather as part of the process God would have us go through in making mature, responsible decisions. This is not to suggest that we must be completely assured of our competence in advance and that we must be able to handle every minor duty of a vocation before entering it; in most cases, there will still be plenty of room for trusting God for further development. But we must at least be certain we have the capacity to develop the basic skills needed in the vocation, if we do not already possess those skills. We should trust that God would make any exception to this abundantly clear through supernatural guidance.. Otherwise, we should assume he will guide us into areas where we can use the gifts and abilities we already have.

When Is a Gift Not a Guide?

Knowing that God will normally lead me only into vocational areas in which I already show some aptitude may not answer all of my questions. How do I know when a particular gift or ability indicates God's call to a vocation? Within the context of Christian fellowship I am to invest my energies in order to meet the needs of my brothers and sisters in Christ. But what about the broader question of long-range vocational commitments? When should I assume that a particular gift or ability is an indication from God to pursue the vocation? If I find, for instance, that I have a definite gift for public speaking, would this indicate the pulpit ministry, or public relations? Or if I enjoy tinkering with electricity, does this mean I am to become an electrical contractor?

Here we have to say that a gift or ability in and of itself never has to be taken as a vocational calling. This should be obvious because most of us have more areas of potential than we could ever pursue. We will always be forced to make choices between various abilities, investing in one at the expense of another. Our gifts and abilities are simply one factor to be considered along with others in guidance. Another vital consideration is whether I desire to use a particular talent. To this should be added my assessment of the opportunities before me and how other people counsel me. These will be discussed in chapters twelve and thirteen.

But another key question remains: Is it necessary for me as a Christian to choose a profession or job which makes obvious use of a spiritual gift? Here I will say two things. On the one hand, it is very clear from Scripture that each of us has a responsibility to make use of spiritual gifts. 1 Peter 4:10 states, "As each has received a gift, employ it for one another, as good stewards of God's varied grace." There is no question that most of us as Christians do not begin to take this responsibility as seriously as we should.

But on the other hand there is nothing in Scripture which commands us to choose a profession or job merely because it provides the opportunity to make direct use of a spiritual gift. We should, in fact, see that such a requirement would actually hurt Christ's ministry rather than benefit it. If we chose our professions on the basis of the opportunities they provide to use spiritual gifts, we would all be inclined to choose "Christian" jobs such as the pastorate, missionary work or teaching in a Christian school.

In general the best rule of thumb is simply to pursue the occupation I most desire to pursue. If this happens to allow me to use a spiritual gift, then fine. But if I would rather work in a department store than be a pastor, it would be a mistake to enter the pastorate simply because that is the most "spiritual" job that challenges my gift for administration. I would do better to enter business and trust that God will still give me a ministry. That ministry will occur through my being a channel of Christ to meet the temporal needs of people, a vital aspect of Christ's purpose on earth. And I may well discover that within the context of the secular business world I will be given a special gift for bringing others to Christ.

Once we find the vocational field we most desire, we should continually look to Christ to give us a fruitful ministry in our daily work, and we must be open to whatever gifts for ministry he might want to give us in that context. Likewise, we must continue to seek every opportunity within a local church or fellowship to use our spiritual gifts in direct service to those in the body of Christ.

Assessing Open and Closed Doors

12

UP TO THIS POINT I have discussed desires and abilities, which refer to everything *about myself* I must consider in making a decision. Now it will help to look at those things *outside myself* which I must consider, in other words, my circumstances.

Actually, we have two types of circumstances. Constraining circumstances prevent us from taking certain actions either through physical force or through making our line of duty extremely plain. A house on fire leaves me little choice but to get out of it; a flat tire on a trip forces me to stop and repair it. Many of our circumstances are of this nature, and they may help simplify our decision making. In some instances closed doors are God's way of showing us that we must sacrifice otherwise worthwhile desires. If I am unemployed and waiting for a particular type of job, but my family runs out of money in the process, I should trust that God would have me at least temporarily settle for a less appealing job in order to keep my family from going hungry.

We also run into nonconstraining circumstances, which offer us opportunities to which we can freely respond or not. If I am considering a certain profession, for instance, and the job market is wide open, I may wonder whether this is a sign from God for me to move ahead or merely a diversion from Satan to sidetrack me. Or, if the job market is unfavorable, I may wonder whether this is God's way of telling me not to enter the profession or whether he might want me to grow in faith by moving ahead in the face of these unfavorable circumstances.

Actually we face these sorts of dilemmas in practically every major decision we make; interpreting circumstances is almost always a problem if we are thinking as deeply as we should. Unfortunately, there is no ultimate way of removing all confusion in this area, and we must recognize that circumstances can have radically different significance in different decisions, depending upon God's purpose for us at the time. If, for instance, God wishes to deepen my trust in him, he might want me to make a decision in the face of less than favorable circumstances. But if, on the other hand, he wants to move me in a direction I would probably not consider going, he might do this through closing off all the other possible alternatives and providing a wide-open door.

Ultimately, the area of circumstances more than any other factor in guidance shows our need to be yielded to Christ and in communion with him through Bible study and prayer. If we are yielded, we may trust that God will guide our decisions, as Romans 12:1-2 promises. In major decisions there is simply no way of knowing the implication of circumstances with unbending certainty, and only as we yield ourselves to God's will can we expect to evaluate these circumstances correctly.

There are, however, two basic principles which I believe can reduce our confusion in this area significantly and make it easier to recognize God's leading. As these principles refer to the role of circumstances in major and minor decisions, it will be helpful to look at each of these areas separately.

Circumstances and Major Decisions

In a major decision (a decision for a vocation) circumstances should play only a limited role in discerning God's will. At best, we should let them play either a suggestive or confirming role.

By *suggestive role* I mean letting circumstances suggest a possibility which should then be judged on the basis of desire, ability and the counsel of others. If, for instance, I am considering going to college, and a university offers me a generous scholarship, there would be good reason to consider this circumstance as God's leading to attend the school. But it would be wrong to take this encouraging circumstance as guidance *in and of itself.* Only if after carefully considering the matter I conclude that I really want to attend the college and would profit from its training should I then decide to enroll there.

By *confirming role* I mean letting circumstances confirm a choice we already have good reasons to think might be God's will. If, for instance, I desire to marry a certain woman, and I believe we would complement each other, then I have reason to think God might be leading toward marriage. But I should not finally conclude this until I ask her to marry me and she accepts. This would be the confirming circumstance. (In a real sense, of course, circumstances must always play a confirming role in our knowledge of God's will; whatever we might suspect God's will to be, we can know with certainty only when he confirms the possibility through circumstances.)

By saying we should limit the role of circumstances to suggestion or confirmation we are really saying something quite important, for as Christians we too often attach undue significance to circumstances, regarding them uncritically as an infallible indicator of God's will. There is a tendency to do this when circumstances are quite favorable, especially when circumstances are highly coincidental, and I find again and again that Christians want to regard such circumstances as God's clear leading without considering any further factors.

As an extreme example, I know of a Christian couple who decided God was leading them to marry because they first met in Europe and then later happened to encounter each other in a church in America. Since they had not made any plans to get together again after their first meeting, this unexpected encounter in America was taken as God's direct guidance to get married. Unfortunately they did not take the time necessary to find out if they were really suited to be married to one another, and not surprisingly they were divorced less than a year after the wedding.

I believe in this instance the mistake came in taking circumstances as divine guidance. While the coincidental meeting certainly gave them good reason to consider further possibilities for their relationship, it was wrong to make as dramatic a move as marriage without a more thorough consideration of their capacities for living together.

In saying this I realize we leave a major area unresolved. We are saying that circumstances should not be taken in and of themselves as guidance, while also saying that they should play a role in our search to know God's will. But to what extent, then, must circumstances appear favorable in advance of the decision we are considering? To what extent must they confirm our desires and abilities *before* we move ahead? Obviously they must always eventually confirm our choices, but to what extent must they do so *in advance?*

Here, unfortunately, there is no pat answer. While in a major decision desire and ability must normally be present to indicate guidance, the degree to which circumstances must appear favorable in advance cannot be stated as a general principle, and it will vary greatly from decision to decision. On the one hand, we can say that if circumstances are in strong agreement with desire and ability, this is a good indication of guidance. But on the other hand, even when they do not seem in agreement, it might still be God's will to move ahead, especially if desire and ability are strong. There is no easy formula for resolving this dilemma.

I wish it were possible to provide a more helpful insight for evaluating circumstances in major decisions, but this is where we really reach our limit in what can reasonably be said about divine guidance. We can say how circumstances should *not* function in these decisions, and this is helpful in narrowing our focus. But the light we can shed from a positive angle is limited.

Open Doors and Minor Decisions

In the area of minor decisions (that is, decisions within a vocation), we should see circumstances as playing a much more defined role. In fact, whereas circumstances should play only a limited role in major decisions, in minor decisions they are God's primary means of conveying his will.

In a major decision we decide for a particular vocation. This decision may be quite complex and the role of circumstances in the decision rather ambiguous. But once the decision is resolved and a commitment made to the vocation, the role of circumstances becomes much clearer. Through the circumstances of the vocations to which we commit ourselves God shows his will for our everyday decisions.

This is vital, for we have a tendency as Christians to overspiritualize minor decisions—to look for some dramatic sign or spiritual impulse to resolve the most insignificant matters. But we need to see that once we have resolved a major area of commitment, God will seldom give us guidance which takes us out of the clear course of that commitment. We must trust that the responsibilities entailed by the commitment are by definition a part of his will.

This principle was a central theme of the Reformation doctrine of vocation, and one which we too quickly lose sight of today. Martin Luther referred to the details of a Christian's vocation as a "daily sermon."[1] We should think of God as virtually preaching his will to us through the responsibilities of our vocations. We need not look further for guidance.

By the same token, we should assume that any opportunity

which is not clearly related to a vocation we have chosen and which might distract us from our present commitment is probably not God's leading. We should trust that if God wants to divert us from responsibilities to which we are already committed, he will make this strikingly clear.

For me the decision to become a pastor in St. Louis was a difficult one. But once it was resolved, much of God's will was clearly defined by it. There was the weekly sermon to write, people needing counsel, hospital visits to make, various programs to plan and other responsibilities clearly implied by the commitment. It would have been foolish for me to expect God to make his will more plain to me than this. And it would have been foolish for me to look beyond these responsibilities to find God's will. If a friend offered me an intriguing business opportunity, I would have known that it simply was not God's will, since it would divert me from my pastoral commitment.

I realize that this principle does not make all minor decisions simple. It does not tell us what to do when faced with conflicting responsibilities within a vocation or between vocations. Deciding between conflicting responsibilities will often be difficult. God may allow many conflicting opportunities to come our way so that we may learn how to make intelligent decisions and to trust him to do what we cannot do.

By showing that normally we do not need to look beyond the obvious responsibilities of our vocations for guidance, this principle narrows our focus in discerning God's will. This does not mean, however, that we are rigidly locked into a vocation once we have chosen it. If we find circumstances extremely unfavorable, then we might have reason to change our situation. But until we have made a responsible decision to leave a vocation, we should assume that its details are a daily sermon—clear guidance and a precious trust from God.

Weighing
the Counsel
of Others

13

WE HAVE DISCUSSED the roles of desires, abilities and circumstances in knowing the will of God. But there is a remaining
factor in decision making—the counsel of other people.
Counsel should play a key role in practically all of our major
decisions and many of our minor decisions as well.

It is sometimes assumed in Christian circles that we are each
in various authority relationships where one person's counsel
is to be taken as God's will by definition. We might refer to this
as a "chain-of-command" relationship. Regardless of what
other factors might seem to suggest, this person's counsel is
considered the final word in knowing God's will. Because this
is an important issue with many Christians, and because the
Bible has some important teachings in this area, we will devote
the appendix to this subject.

In this chapter, however, we will look at the more general
aspects of counsel, as this is a concern to all of us. Those interested in the specific subject of chain-of-command relation-

ships will want to work through the study in the appendix.

Members of a Body

The great tragedy of evangelical Christianity has been a tendency toward individualism. We have tended to stress our relationship with Christ to the exclusion of our relationships with other Christians. We have emphasized commitment to Christ as the only essential in the Christian life and fellowship as a nicety but not a necessity. We think of fellowship as potluck dinners and other social events rather than as the building of significant personal relationships. The result has been a pietistic sort of Christianity where even though we spend time together as Christians we are isolated from one another in the deeper matters of life, reluctant to share struggles and important decisions with each other.

When we turn to the New Testament, we find a strikingly different picture of Christian community. In the early church, commitment to Jesus Christ was not thought of apart from commitment to one another—the two notions were inseparable. The church was understood as the body of Christ, and to be committed to Jesus Christ, the head, meant also to be committed to his body, the company of those who believe in him. Thus we find John saying, "he who does not love his brother [in Christ] whom he has seen, cannot love God whom he has not seen" (1 Jn. 4:20). And we often find Paul talking about love for Christ and love for fellow believers in the same breath (for example, see 2 Thess. 1:3; Col. 1:4; 2 Cor. 8:3-5; Philem. 4-5). When we observe the examples of Christian community described in Acts 2:41-47 and elsewhere, we see an infectious sort of fellowship between believers who have a familylike closeness.

If we take this New Testament emphasis on fellowship seriously, it should have profound implications for the way we live our lives as Christians. In short, we must realize that we are called to live our lives not only for Jesus Christ but also for one another. This entails an intimate sort of caring for and sharing with one another in all aspects of our lives. Specifically, it should mean that any serious endeavor to know God's will should not be an isolated effort but one shared with other Christians. If my commitment to Christ is inseparable from my commitment to other believers, then I must not expect to fully understand his will apart from being in relationship with other Christians, and I should expect that he would often convey his will to me through others. I should regard any attempt to resolve an important decision without the counsel of other Christians as a short circuit of my relationship with Christ.

It is important that we have regular involvement in Christian fellowship. This is vital to our spiritual health in all areas, and especially to gaining the desire to do God's will. We will find that through regular fellowship with other Christians our thinking in many areas becomes clarified. We stressed in chapter eleven how this happens, for instance, in the area of spiritual gifts. Sometimes we will find that simply through casual dialog with others we discover strengths and weaknesses in ourselves which were hidden to us but which have a bearing on a decision with which we are wrestling. The spiritual stimulation in fellowship is such that it inevitably has a positive influence on our thought processes.

When we are faced with a major decision it is especially important to go to other Christians and share this decision quite openly, seeking their thoughts and reflections on it. As believers we do not take this responsibility seriously enough. Not only does the New Testament emphasis on fellowship give us a strong mandate to seek counsel in our decision making, but this also makes good sense for purely practical reasons. It is our nature as human creatures that dialog on a subject stimulates us to think more deeply about it. There is a certain chemistry in the process of communication that invariably broadens our thinking, even if talking things over adds nothing new to our understanding of the problem. From this angle we can see that verbalization in and of itself—

whether with a Christian or not—is generally a healthy process.

Thus, in the practical admonitions of Proverbs we find the importance of seeking counsel a recurring theme:

Where there is no guidance, a people falls; but in an abundance of counselors there is safety. (11:14)

The way of a fool is right in his own eyes, but a wise man listens to advice. (12:15)

Without counsel plans go wrong, but with many advisers they succeed. (15:22)

Listen to advice and accept instruction, that you may gain wisdom for the future. (19:20)

The purpose in a man's mind is like deep water, but a man of understanding will draw it out. (20:5)

Plans are established by counsel; by wise guidance wage war. (20:18)

By wise guidance you can wage your war, and in abundance of counselors there is victory. (24:6)

Iron sharpens iron, and one man sharpens another. (27:17)[1]

All in all, then, we must conclude from both theological and practical standpoints that counsel is indispensable to responsible Christian decision making. We must see counsel as one of God's prime channels of guidance.

Assimilating Advice

In stressing the importance of counsel, we need also to point out the particular role it should play in our decision making. We need to understand how to evaluate the recommendations we receive in light of God's will. Should we suppose that if counsel from many people points unanimously in a certain direction, this is where God is leading? Or what if the advice we receive is contradictory?

With the exception of certain chain-of-command situations (discussed in the appendix), I do not believe we are ever under obligation to regard any counsel as God's will by definition, regardless of how many people might agree with the advice and regardless of the spiritual maturity of the one giving it. The value of counsel, in my opinion, lies not in providing direct insight into God's will, but in the fact that through counsel a healthy mental process occurs in which we are inspired to think more creatively, to see new alternatives and to see old alternatives in a new light. The end result is a deeper understanding of the issues at stake in our decisions. Ultimately, we must make our own decision in light of our desires, abilities and circumstances, even if it flies in the face of the counsel we have received.

When we consider the proverbs listed on the previous page, we find that none say we must accept counsel as divine leading. When the proverbs stress that there is strength in a multitude of counselors, for instance, there is no suggestion that the strength comes from the content of the counsel. There is little indication that from the counsel of many people a certain course of action will be advised which will be the direction we must take. The proverbs are not that specific. They stress that there is an advantage to many advisers and imply that through counseling we are helped to think more deeply, and we are strengthened to make wiser decisions.

I believe, to be sure, that if a large number of people concur in their advice, we should seriously consider whether it is not indeed God's will. The burden of proof should be on us to show why it is not God's leading. But we need to remember that there are many times in Scripture where one person was right and the multitude wrong. As adults we are not ultimately obliged to look on any counsel as the will of God, but merely as a help from God in responsibly thinking through our decisions.

By the same token, as mature Christians we should not lean on other people to make our decisions for us. While God gives us counsel as a help in understanding his will, he never wants it to become a crutch. We must remember that he expects us to grow through taking responsibility for our own decisions.

Obtaining Counsel

In addition to talking about how to evaluate counsel, we need to say something about how we should go about seeking counsel when making an important decision. From what sort of persons should we seek counsel, and how many should we consult?

It is difficult to lay down hard and fast rules at this point. The type of counsel we should seek will vary greatly from decision to decision and from person to person. But I believe there are some general guidelines we can mention which are helpful to follow.

1. Seek counsel only when making a major decision or one which requires significant deliberation. Minor decisions normally will not require seeking counsel.

2. Consult more people on more momentous decisions. The more critical the choice, the greater should be the number of persons from whom counsel is sought. In deciding on a major in college or a particular course of vocational training, for instance, you might ask the advice of a dozen people who would be likely to take your decision seriously. On deciding whether or not to teach a Sunday-school class or sit on a church committee, only a close friend's advice might be needed.

3. Seek counsel from a variety of persons, including those you do not expect will agree with you. The purpose of advice is not to simply confirm a decision you've already made.

4. Give greater emphasis to getting counsel from Christians than from non-Christians, because the former are part of the body of Christ through whom God gives special insight into his will. Also, from a practical standpoint, Christians are more likely to identify with the spiritual aspects of your decision.

5. Get counsel from those who know you particularly well, such as parents, other family members, close friends and so on. If you are married, priority should be on the counsel of your spouse, and there should normally be strong agreement between you and your spouse on any major decision.

6. Consult spiritual leaders with whom you are in contact. Find a pastor, chaplain, Inter-Varsity staff member or other Christian leader whom you feel can be trusted with the confidence of your decision.

7. Seek counsel from a psychologist, psychiatrist or other person specially trained in counseling if your decision is causing you particular emotional difficulties. Big decisions can be expected to cause you a certain amount of anxiety. But if your emotions prevent you from making a rational decision or carrying that decision through, it might be best to talk to a professional counselor. A pastor, teacher or friend might be able to advise you on who to see.

In laying down guidelines for seeking counsel, one word of caution is perhaps in order. We cannot go on endlessly getting counsel for any particular decision. We reach a point where seeking counsel amounts to an escape from dealing head-on with our problems. The fear of taking responsibility for our decisions can lead us to seek counsel in an effort to delay the decision or perhaps in the hope of being persuaded to depart from what we see to be our clear line of duty. While there is no easy way of judging just when this point has been reached, the important thing is to be alert to the danger and to be praying for wisdom and balance in the whole process.

For most of us, however, I believe the danger lies, not in seeking too much counsel, but in not taking the need for counsel seriously enough. We must forever fight the tendency to think that we have a private pipeline to God and can discover his will for our lives without the help of others. God has made us as social creatures, who find identity and purpose only in relationships with other people. And we cannot expect to understand God's direction in our lives apart from the experience of sharing our lives and decisions with those who bear his image on this earth.

Finally
Deciding
14

WE HAVE COVERED quite a few bases in this whole subject of knowing God's will. Hopefully the study has not served to confuse you further but has helped clear up some areas of misunderstanding in the matter of guidance.

We began by setting forth our intention to look at the subject of God's will for *complex decisions,* that is, those unique personal decisions which cannot be resolved simply through the application of biblical moral principles. We noted further that our knowledge of God's will must be thought of not as prophetic insight into the future, but as a mature grasp of his immediate desire for a present decision. We then devoted a chapter to emphasizing the enormous initiative that God takes in guidance and the fact that our search for God's will should always be undertaken with the assurance that God is much more concerned with our doing his will than we could ever be.

We said that our first responsibility in knowing God's will

was to be willing to do it. If we are willing, then we may be confident that God will not allow us to miss his will, regardless of our confusion over it. Prayer is the key to developing and maintaining this willingness. With an attitude of prayerful willingness, we should seek whatever light Scripture throws on our decision. Then we can proceed to do a careful, rational analysis of the decision, trusting that as we look for the alternative that appears most to glorify Christ, he will see that we have the evidence we need to choose that alternative. In particular, in making a major decision, we should look at the factors of personal desires, abilities, circumstances and the counsel of others.

The Proof Is in the Person

Up to this point we have talked quite theoretically. We have discussed what *should be* done or what *can be* done, so that by now our heads are swimming with information. But some readers might protest that all of this is easier said than done, and we have not looked at how this advice can actually be put to use. In concluding, then, let us take a look at a couple of hypothetical cases.

First, let us look at the case of Jamie. When Jamie entered the university, her intention was to become a missionary doctor. Her decision had been based not on desire as much as on a sense of obligation. Her father was a surgeon, and ever since she could remember her family had encouraged her to pursue a medical career. Also, she had long been a member of a church which had put an unhealthy emphasis on denying natural aspirations. You should enter a profession mainly for the opportunity it presents to serve others, she had been taught, even if this means doing the very thing you do not want to do.

While she was in high school, a missionary nurse spoke to Jamie's youth group. The woman's presentation was inspiring, and Jamie found herself becoming excited about the prospect of missionary medical service. "Surely God must want me to do this," she thought. From then on, she simply assumed that God had called her to enter the field, even though she increasingly doubted that this was what she really desired to do.

Jamie's first year in college was a sobering experience. She found her zoology and chemistry courses uninteresting and the required memorization tedious. Her grades were poor, and more and more she dreaded going to class. During her second semester, however, she decided to try an elective course in accounting. She discovered a genuine interest in the subject, and while other students struggled with the material, she grasped it well.

During the summer she took a job with an accounting firm. She enjoyed the work immensely and found the business environment stimulating. The following semester she took a standard interest test at the vocational counseling center of her university. It revealed a distinct interest in the areas of business analysis and management and minimal interest in medical work.

At this point Jamie sought counsel from a campus minister. She shared with him that she felt a growing interest in pursuing an accounting career but feared that God had already given his final word on her profession. She also admitted that she felt extremely guilty about entering a profession she enjoyed so much. The campus minister explained to her that God had not made her the way she was by accident. He showed her various passages of Scripture which suggested that her interests and potential were a strong sign of God's vocational direction. He also explained that she was under no obligation to regard the sense of inspiration she had felt during the missionary's talk as a final call from God. "God may have used your thoughts about a medical career to bring you to this college where you would find out that you should be an accountant," he suggested.

Jamie left the session considerably relieved and with a new sense of freedom in Christ to follow a profession that suited her personality. Upon graduation she found employment as an accountant with a hospital. Her background had uniquely suited her to employ her business skills within a medical environment. Her managerial skills were also noticed by her supervisors, and eventually she was promoted to a management position.

In another situation God might use the same factors in Jamie's background to lead someone else into a career of medical missions. But then the person's temperament would probably be clearly inclined in that direction. In any case, a person in a similar situation would have the right and responsibility to consider his or her personality make-up a vital indication of God's leading.

Making the First Move

John's case is also interesting. Through studying the biblical teaching on the role of church leaders and carefully considering his interests and abilities, he concluded that he could productively serve Christ as a pastor. He took this to be God's will and negotiated the first steps toward this goal by attending seminary. Then John faced the complex question of where and in what way God wanted him to serve.

This is a problem for any high-school or college graduate entering the job market for the first time. It is one thing to follow a particular course of study because you believe that is where God wants you. But facing the realities of the job market can be a great strain on your faith. We must not underestimate this problem for seminary graduates either. In many denominations, for instance, there is no organized system of placement, so one must simply depend upon being chosen by a particular congregation.

John was a member of such a denomination and was without a job offer. Graduation was coming up in three months. John wrestled with the very real question of what was God's responsibility and what was his in this matter. He knew he must pray earnestly for God's direction. But beyond this, would faith demand that he do nothing but wait patiently and trust that God would drop the ideal opportunity into his lap? Or would this be presumptuous? Should he instead take the initiative himself by following the practical steps taken by most other people who are looking for jobs?

Although less than fully convinced, he finally decided on the latter course, partly out of restlessness, and partly because he felt it would be lazy not to make some effort toward finding employment. He filled out his denomination's complicated dossier, contacted the seminary placement office, and then sent his résumé to churches with open positions. While John was open to a wide range of possibilities in the area of pastoral work, he had concluded through long and prayerful consideration that because of his interest in preaching the most ideal job would include a regular opportunity to preach. Likewise, because he had been successful in working with college students, he felt it would be especially good if he could serve a church located near a university. Yet, recognizing that the job market was quite crowded and that he must be open to new areas into which the Lord might lead him, John sent his résumé to a large variety of churches.

John continued his daily devotional time and prayed for God's wisdom and grace in the matter of finding pastoral work. But by graduation time he had contacted more than fifty churches with no positive response. Two weeks after graduation, however, an extraordinary coincidence occurred. He received an encouraging letter from a friend in Detroit from whom he had not heard in over a year. Then on the next day a church in Detroit to which he had sent his dossier called him and asked him to visit as a candidate. His immediate response was that surely this coincidence was a sign from God that he should go to Detroit.

But a pastor friend encouraged him to take a close look at the situation first. As he did, John discovered that the church wanted him to serve primarily as a youth assistant with limited opportunities for preaching. Also, there would be little chance to minister to college students. He knew in his heart that he was open to going there if Christ wanted him to go. But from the evidence he had he concluded that this situation would not be a wise investment of his potential nor a challenging atmosphere for growth. He cautiously decided not to go, but asked Christ to make it clear if he was wrong.

Then a week later another invitation came, this time from a church in Richmond, Virginia, which had heard about John through the seminary placement office. From the phone call John found out that the church was located several blocks from a university and provided an outstanding location for college ministry. In addition, as an assistant, John would be expected to preach regularly in the Sunday evening service. John then made a further, careful investigation of the situation by phoning a friend in Richmond who had attended this church for some time.

John also sought counsel from several friends and pastors. Finally, he flew to Richmond to candidate officially at the church and spent several days there. He enjoyed the people of the church and felt they were open to his ideas and gifts. At the end of his visit they gave him an official "call." After a couple more days of thinking, praying and reading the Word, John accepted the call.

From Jamie's and John's experiences we can learn several things. The first inquiry John received, from the church in Detroit, was a classic example of a coincidental circumstance, since he had received an unrelated letter from a friend there on the preceding day. And John's immediate reaction was a typical one—to assume God was giving special guidance through the coincidence. But, on the advice of others, John backed up and took a second look. When he did he logically concluded that the opportunity did not reasonably fit his interests and abilities, and he turned it down. It was only his first "nibble"; there would be others. To have looked on the coincidental circumstance as extraordinary guidance would have been an unfortunate assumption.

In a similar manner, Jamie was encouraged not to assume that her feelings during the missionary's presentation were an indication of God's will. Instead, she took a more careful look at her interests and abilities and made a decision based on them.

John may be commended for making a mature and responsible effort to investigate the Richmond church before finally responding to the invitation. But what comes through loud and clear is that God took an amazing amount of responsibility for guidance. He brought John to a position which he had not even sought (John had not sent his résumé to the church in Virginia), and it turned out to be ideal. This did much to deepen John's trust in Christ.

Still a hard question remains: Were John and Jamie wrong to try hard to find the right job and the right major? Would they have shown greater faith if they had just sat still and waited for God to bring things about? We must say no. In John's case, the preparation of the résumé itself was clearly worthwhile, as this was the information which the Richmond church received from the placement office. Beyond this, even though no positive response came from sending the résumés out, this effort allowed him to accept the Richmond call with the assurance that he had reasonably covered the bases elsewhere and was not being impulsive in accepting the position.

I would like to suggest that there is truth in the adage: God cannot steer a parked car. In many cases I believe that God waits until he sees us taking responsibility before he brings the right opportunity along, even though that opportunity might not be directly related to our personal efforts. God did not force Jamie into an accounting major. She first tried out a course in the subject, then took a summer job in business. She made the moves and God used them to reveal his will.

All of this is not to imply, of course, that God does not sometimes make the process of finding his will considerably easier or harder than it was for Jamie and John. Unlike Jamie, some college students are sure of exactly what they want to do when they begin college. And they stick to that goal through their four years. Others change majors in college or courses of study in high school several times before settling on one interest. Some seminary graduates receive offers before they ever start to look; others who are very qualified look for six months or a year before receiving a call. There is no normal pattern.

God's ways of leading different persons are drastically different. Jamie's and John's experiences are simply examples of the correct approach to seeking God's will. When we are faced with a decision where God's will is not clear, whether in employment or any other area, we must normally expect that he wants us to take some initiative to figure it out. This is part of our process of maturing in Christ.

The Abundant Life Is Not an Easy One

Some Christians believe that as we grow in Christ we should find it easier and easier to recognize his will. In one sense this is obviously true. The more we learn about how Christ guides, the less time we will spend looking for his guidance in the wrong ways. But from another angle we may well find the reverse to be true. Growing in Christ means growing in responsibility, and as he sees that we are able to handle it, he allows us greater and greater responsibility. This means that we will have a greater part in decision making and that the decisions God allows us to tackle may in many cases be more difficult rather than less so.

This has been a common experience among people who have lived their lives for Christ on the growing edge. D. E. Hoste, for instance, refers to a conversation with Hudson Taylor, one of the greatest missionaries in recent history: "We were talking about guidance. He said how in his younger days, things used to come so clearly, so quickly to him. 'But,' he said, 'now as I have gone on, and God has used me more and more, I seem often to be like a man going along in a fog. I do not know what to do.' "[1]

This is not to imply that God ever wants his will to be hope-lessly enigmatic to us. It is merely to emphasize that as we grow in Christ, he often makes us more accountable for our own decisions than we were when we were younger in the faith. We should welcome this opportunity, for it means a maturing in Christ which can come no other way.

And we can have complete confidence that whether we feel God's guiding presence or not, he remains every bit as near, giving us all the direction we need to walk in the path of his will. God's will is not simply meant to be discerned, it is meant to be *affirmed.* As we seek through prayer a heart that longs for his will and devote the best of our rational efforts toward finding his will, we may make the decisions of life with great conviction that he is guiding them. While there is never room for the presumptuous spirit which thinks it has a final grasp on God's will, neither is there room for the faint-hearted spirit which is afraid to make decisions and to trust Christ for guidance in them.

My prayer is that you would receive from this book not only a deeper understanding of the principles of knowing God's will, but also a spirit of courage to make decisions when they must be made, trusting Christ that even when the answer does not seem obvious, he is working out his will through the mind that seeks it and the heart that is truly open to him.

Authority
Relationships
and the
Will of God

In this section we want to look at the biblical teaching on authority. In chapter thirteen, on counsel, we showed that counsel should play an important role in finding God's will. We stressed that it should function as advice and as stimulation for our thinking, but not as a final authority in our decisions. We are left, however, with the question of whether there are certain relationships where final authority exists (that is, so-called chain-of-command relationships where one person's counsel is taken without question to be God's will). Some Christians, for instance, believe that an unmarried person should follow the counsel of his or her parents, and married women should be led by the counsel of their husbands in all matters.

Obviously we must always be in certain limited authority relationships, such as with employers, teachers and civil authorities. But authority here does not generally extend beyond a restricted area, and certainly not to our important personal decisions. Furthermore, these relationships ordinarily can be broken at will. A chain-of-command relationship, however, is a binding one, where there is final authority even over major life decisions.

In popular thinking there are three relationships where this sort of authority is often believed to exist: the relationships between parents and children, husbands and wives, and of spiritual leaders with those under them. Although Christians by no means agree on their views in any of these areas, in each case there are many who believe the Scriptures teach a hierarchy of authority. We need, then, to give close attention to the biblical teachings on each of these relationships to determine what role, if any, strict authority should play in them.

Parents and Children

The issue of obedience to parents has left many Christians confused in recent years. Bill Gothard, in his popular seminar, "Institute in Basic Youth Conflicts," has laid considerable stress on the obedience due from the Christian child even to non-Christian parents.[1] Other Christian teachers have countered that the Christian child is free in Christ to make his or her own decisions. While the counsel of parents should be respected, it is not binding.

To come to grips with the biblical teaching on this matter, we will look at Ephesians 6:1-4 and Colossians 3:20-21, as these are the most explicit statements in the Bible about the obedience due to parents, and they are the passages most often quoted in support of parental authority:

> Children, obey your parents in the Lord, for this is right. "Honor your father and mother" (this is the first commandment with a promise), "that it may be well with you and that you may live long on the earth." Fathers, do not provoke your children to anger, but bring them up in the discipline and instruction of the Lord. (Eph. 6:1-4)

> Children, obey your parents in everything, for this pleases the Lord. Fathers, do not provoke your children, lest they become discouraged. (Col. 3:20-21)

Both of these passages obviously give strong support to parental authority.

To begin with, the type of obedience Paul is talking about in these verses is absolute: children are to obey parents "in everything" (Col. 3:20). While Paul would surely make an exception if the parent commanded the child to sin,[2] it does not appear that any other exception would be entertained. In all other cases the child should simply assume that his or her parents' wishes indicate the will of God. The phrase *in the Lord* in Ephesians 6:1 does not, I believe, indicate that parents are to be obeyed only when their counsel appears to be the Lord's leading. I would agree with T. K. Abbott that this phrase is not to be taken "as defining the limits of obedience . . . but rather showing the spirit in which the obedience is to be yielded."[3] Paul is saying that obedience is to be rendered in a reverent spirit.

In addition, Paul does not seem to be making any distinction between Christian and non-Christian parents in these passages. He does not say that one must obey only Christian parents. And while it might be thought that he assumed only children of Christian parents would read the Epistles,[4] this seems unlikely, for it appears that many children of unbelieving parents would have become Christians in the early years of the church. Also, in

Romans 1:30 and 2 Timothy 3:2 Paul expressed disgust with the disobedience to parents present in pagan society, showing that he viewed obedience to parents as a human virtue irrespective of a family's religious status. Thus it appears that the command to obey parents is to be followed by all children, regardless of their parents' Christian commitment. Children should assume that their parents' counsel indicates God's will, even though their parents might not have the slightest concern about what God would will.

But while the passages support parental authority at these points, at another point they force us to qualify strongly the chain-of-command notion. The passages do not say that any unmarried person is to render this obedience to parents, but that it is due from *children*. "*Children*, obey your parents" (italics added). There is a chronological distinction here which is overlooked by many Christians. The Greek word for children (*ta tekna*) used in these passages indicates not any son or daughter, but a person who is still dependent.[5]

This is a crucial distinction to make, for it shows that the unmarried adult is no longer under the obligation of these verses, for that person by definition is no longer a child. Also it suggests that for young people in the later teens the chain-of-command requirement is less clearly defined. Most young people today go through a transitional stage between being a dependent child and a self-supporting adult. During this stage their parental dependence gradually lessens. The person, for instance, who leaves home for college right after high school may still have strong financial dependence upon his or her parents, but may be forced into a new independence in many other areas. It would certainly be wrong to think of such a person as a child. This person is in a more ambiguous state where childish dependence is decreasing and adult self-reliance increasing. Thus, while a college student should continue to value greatly the counsel of his or her parents, the student should not feel obligated to regard their advice as God's will by definition. Also, from a practical standpoint, the person in such a transitional state will never develop the maturity to make independent decisions if he or she continues to rely solely on parental counsel. A weaning period must occur, simply for the sake of personal growth.

Exactly where this transitional stage begins cannot be laid down with any rigidity. Most young people probably reach it somewhere in high school, and Christian parents should generally by tenth or eleventh grade begin to encourage their children to take greater and greater responsibility for their own decisions. I would think that normally children in the early high-school years should continue to think of themselves as children with respect to the biblical commands, and trust that their parents' wishes convey God's will.

In summary, then, the chain-of-command relationship exists between parents and children, but ceases during the adolescent years when the child begins making adult decisions. This does not belittle the importance of parental counsel for those beyond the chain-of-command stage. As Christians—regardless of age or marital status—the command to honor our parents always applies, and this certainly suggests that we should give serious consideration to their counsel. Our parents are often much better equipped to understand and counsel us than we give them credit for. Generally, I believe the burden of proof rests on us to show why we should not follow our parents' advice in a particular major decision.

But no adult or later adolescent needs to feel that his or her parents' advice must be taken as God's will if other factors clearly point in a different direction. To follow parental direction in such an instance could be to put parents above Christ, a tendency we are warned against in Luke 14:26 and elsewhere. Ultimately we must accept the fact that Christ has called us to a life of responsible thinking, and we must beware lest we rely too heavily on our parents to make our decisions for us.

Husbands and Wives

There are two prevailing views among Christians today about the interpretation of New Testament teachings on order in marriage. These often result in different ideas about authority in the marriage relationship. In various passages a pattern of authority is set forth: the husband is declared head of the wife as Christ is head of the church (for instance, Eph. 5:21-33; Col. 3:18-19) and as Abraham was master of Sarah (1 Pet. 3:1-7). Thus, the wife is to submit to her husband. Many Christians feel that these statements are to be interpreted as God's command for hierarchy in marriage today and that no cultural considerations will affect their meaning and application. This has been the traditional interpretation.

On the other hand, an increasing number of Christians with a high view of biblical authority have concluded that these commands were not meant to be binding for Christians of all times. They were rather intended to correct some unfortunate circumstances in the early churches or as an acquiescence to the culture of that time. Wives were told to submit to their husbands so that Christians would not challenge a social custom in a way that would hinder the spread of the gospel. In the same way Christian women were instructed to wear veils and not to talk during worship.

These commands, it is argued, should be seen in the same class as those about slaves obeying their masters. They had their place in the culture of the first century. But just as we would no longer look upon slavery as God's perfect will, neither should we insist on male headship in marriage as God's ideal. God's highest design for marriage is reflected in Galatians 3:28, where Paul says, "There is neither Jew nor Greek, there is neither slave nor free, there is neither male nor female; for you are all one in Christ Jesus." The unity portrayed in that passage should be understood as touching all aspects of life, not simply the spiritual. Within marriage the ideal pattern is one of partnership, where the husband and wife delegate authority as they choose.

The issues involved in this question are quite complex, and it is well beyond my purposes to go deeply into them or to argue for one side against the other. Much helpful material has been written on both sides, and I would encourage you to study the subject carefully, examine the biblical passages closely, and work through your own position.[6] My only caution would be not to be judgmental of someone who reaches a different conclusion from yours, as the best minds are divided on this matter. It is vital that we maintain respect for each other's viewpoints in this area.

I do want to argue, however, that regardless of which position you hold, there is no basis for a rigid chain-of-command situation. I believe these passages should be seen as presenting a balanced picture of authority. They have sometimes been used to justify situations of extreme male dominance, where the husband is the final authority in all decisions and the wife is always expected passively to accept his opinion. In reality, I see a quite different spirit conveyed.

Paul, for instance, begins his teaching on marriage in Ephesians 5 with the statement, "Be subject to one another out of reverence for Christ" (v. 21). He does not separate the wife's submission to her husband from the thought that the husband must also demonstrate submission to his wife. He goes on to tell husbands to love their wives as Christ loved the church. While Christ was the perfect example of a leader, he was also the perfect servant, and the implications for the husband's role are profound.

Cultural considerations aside, then, Paul is saying that there must be mutual submission within marriage. This is stated perhaps even more plainly in 1 Corinthians 7:4: "For the wife does not rule over her own body, but the husband does; likewise the husband does not rule over his own body, but the wife does." While this verse has obvious reference to the sexual act, it certainly implies the broader principle that husbands and wives have authority to influence their spouse's decisions in all areas.

In addition, we might note that Peter closes his statement on marital order in 1 Peter 3:1-7 by referring to husbands and wives as "joint heirs of the grace of life" (v. 7) and follows with an appeal for unity of spirit (v. 8).

In short, the straightforward teaching of these passages affirms male headship only within the context of mutual submission. Couples who wish to be consistent with this teaching should strive for agreement in their decision making. Regardless of which position is held on the application and interpretation of these passages, one must conclude that discerning God's will in marriage is a mutual matter. While a couple should feel the freedom to delegate in small decisions, certainly in broad vocational decisions there should be agreement before they would consider an alternative to be God's leading.

For the couple that accepts male headship, I would think that it would apply only if after much discussion they find themselves at a genuine impasse, where a decision must be made even though agreement cannot be reached. Then it would be right for the husband's opinion to prevail. But hopefully this would be the rare exception in the normal marriage.

Ordinarily couples should recognize their obligation before Christ to make a concerted effort to reach accord in major decisions. This admittedly can be a painful and prolonged process. It takes much more time and effort than simply letting the husband decide and the wife passively follow. But I do not see any other process as true to the spirit of the Scriptures. The dividends in the long run will be closer companionship between husband and wife and greater sensitivity to the Lord's leading.

Spiritual Leaders

We come finally to the question of the authority of spiritual leaders. Most Christians find themselves in a relationship with one or more so-called spiritual leaders, whether within a church or a fellowship group outside of the church. Inevitably, the question arises, is this person's counsel only to be taken as advice, or does his or her opinion carry special weight by virtue of position?

Interestingly, when we turn to the New Testament we find no evidence that a spiritual leader's counsel should ever be taken as more than advice in major complex decisions. To begin with, there is no clear indication that leaders in the early church were regarded as special interpreters of God's will in such decisions. If we look, for instance, at the various passages regarding the appointment of leaders, we find no evidence that positions of leadership included authority in the area of complex decisions (see Acts 6:1-6; 14:23; 1 Tim. 3:1-13; 5:17-22; Tit. 1:5-10; compare Rom. 12:3-8; 1 Cor. 12; Eph. 4:11-14). The leader was to be respected in decisions regarding the life of the church, to be sure. But there is no indication that the leader's word had to be followed in personal matters such as occupation, marriage and so on. (And even in matters directly pertinent to the church's life it is not evident that the leader's directions were to be taken as God's will beyond question.)

It becomes evident in Acts 15:36-41 that not even the apostles were regarded as infallible interpreters of God's will. When Paul and Barnabas disagreed over the question of taking John Mark with them on further missionary travels, Luke gives no indication that Barnabas was disobedient to God's will because he disagreed with Paul.

It is sometimes claimed that Paul's commands to his disciples to be imitators *(mimētēs)* of him implies that they were expected to obey him in their personal, complex decisions (1 Cor. 4:16; 11:1; Phil. 3:17; 2 Thess. 3:7, 9; compare 1 Thess. 1:6). Willis P. DeBoer, however, in an exhaustive study of these passages concludes, "The primary thought in Paul's speaking of his readers as *mimētai* [imitators] is not that they are obliged to be obedient to him and to act in accordance with his instructions."[7] Paul rather seems to be referring to an imitation of his virtuous lifestyle.

The lack of emphasis upon obedience to spiritual leaders in major personal decisions in the New Testament is strikingly underlined by the fact that while Paul and Peter both set forth very specific statements regarding certain authority relationships, there is no specific command given regarding obedience due to a spiritual leader in these sections (Eph. 5:21 —6:9; Col. 3:18—4:1; 1 Pet. 2:13—3:7).

There are in the New Testament only two passages where a direct command regarding obedience to spiritual leaders is given, Matthew 23:2-3 and Hebrews 13:17. In the former passage Jesus tells his disciples, "The scribes and the Pharisees sit on Moses' seat; so practice and observe whatever they tell you, but not what they do; for they preach, but do not practice." Here Jesus sets forth a command which can rightly be understood as an injunction to respect the authority of religious leaders, whether their behavior is commendable or not. It is doubtful, however, that this command pertains to the area of complex decisions.

Jesus refers to the scribes and Pharisees as sitting on Moses' seat, that is, they were interpreters of the law of Moses. Thus he seems merely to be telling his disciples to follow the laws of the Pentateuch as interpreted to them by the scribes and Pharisees. And even more, he is pointing out how hypocritical the scribes and Pharisees are because they do not practice what they preach. Jesus wants his disciples' lifestyles to conform to the spirit of the law.

The injunction of Hebrews 13:17 is: "Obey your leaders and submit to them; for they are keeping watch over your souls, as men who will have to give account." Here Christians are explicitly commanded to obey their spiritual leaders. And yet the writer of Hebrews does not explain precisely what this obedience involves. It is frankly impossible to know with certainty what he meant. There is, however, no basis for concluding that he necessarily meant an unbending sort of obedience.

We today often use the expression "obey your leader" in situations where obvious parameters are implicit. Thus, a student is told simply, "obey your teacher," even though certain limits to that obedience are understood. If the teacher would give an unreasonable homework assignment, the student would not be expected to comply. Likewise, no matter how strongly the teacher would urge the student to participate in some extracurricular activity, the student would still be free to do as he or she wished.

It is probable, I believe, that the author of Hebrews similarly told his readers to obey their leaders in a limited sense. This is most apparent from the Greek term rendered "obey" in verse 17: it is actually better interpreted, "be persuaded." W. E. Vine comments, "The obedience suggested is not by submission to authority, but resulting from persuasion."[8] If the author had meant to imply a rigid authority in any sense, he surely would have used a stronger term.[9]

I believe that most likely he was merely urging his readers to a general obedience in matters touching the corporate life of the church and that his command had nothing to do with personal complex decisions. Probably his statement was understood by readers in this sense, in the same way that we understand what is meant if someone says, "obey your teacher." Even in this area of the church's corporate life, there is no reason to assume he was implying an absolute authority for the leaders. He was probably just encouraging the readers toward a reasonable measure of respect and submission, which must exist for leaders to function.

Whatever the case, we have to say that if God wanted to convey the fact that Christian leaders should have chain-of-command authority over decisions in any area, it would have been stated more explicitly here or elsewhere. As it is, we have no clear New Testament evidence to this effect. We must conclude that a Christian is not required to regard the counsel of a spiritual leader as the will of God by definition. While we should seek counsel from qualified spiritual leaders in making major personal decisions, we must not feel under any compulsion to regard this counsel uncritically as divine guidance. We may feel free to weigh it along with other factors which appear to be pointing toward God's will.

Chains-of-Command

We have looked at relationships between parents and children, husbands and wives, and spiritual leaders and their followers. We have discovered that the same spirit of reasonable decision making that permeated our discussion of knowing God's will also applies here. Parents are to direct their children's decisions until the children show that they are ready to begin making choices on their own. Husbands and wives, likewise, are to labor together to choose alternatives which seem reasonable to both of them. And we are all to listen with respect to the advice of our spiritual leaders and then to weigh this advice along with other factors to come up with a rational choice. God wants to give us as much responsibility for finding his will as we can handle. He wants us not to be robots for him, but living, thinking, reasoning beings willing to follow his leading.

NOTES

Chapter 1

[1]Joseph Bayly et al., *Essays on Guidance* (Downers Grove, Ill.: Inter-Varsity Press, 1968), preface.

Chapter 2

[1]Look at books on the subject of guidance in Christian bookstores, and you will find in almost every case that the subject is complex decisions, not simple moral issues. The only exception is that some books on guidance also deal with gray area decisions.

[2]The gray area decision, as we have said, is a decision about moral behavior where the Bible clearly leaves us liberty of choice. Paul discusses this area specifically in Romans 14, 1 Corinthians 8 and 1 Corinthians 10:23-33. In these passages there are set forth two basic guidelines for gray area decisions which can often make such decisions simple.

If I have strong reservations of conscience about a certain gray area activity, then I should not participate (Rom. 14:14, 23; 1 Cor. 8:7). Likewise, if my participation would create problems of conscience for another Christian, then I must respect that person's scruples (Rom. 14:13-23; 1 Cor. 8:7-13, 10:23-33). If my friend is offended by my drinking a glass of wine with dinner, for instance, I must at least refrain in his presence.

Our broader complex decisions, however, are seldom that simple.

The fact that my friend is offended by my desire to enter business, for example, does not necessarily tell me a thing. And the significance of my feelings of conscience about such a decision is often more difficult to assess than in a gray area decision. In this book we will be concerned with complex decisions, which normally cannot be resolved simply through the two biblical guidelines for gray areas. In addition, it may be said that gray area decisions which are not affected by the restrictions these guidelines set forth can be regarded as complex decisions. If, in other words, a gray area activity neither causes conscience problems for myself nor for my Christian friends, then I may approach it as I would a complex decision.

³As eminent a Christian as John Wesley followed this approach!

⁴Paul Little, *Affirming the Will of God* (Downers Grove, Ill.: InterVarsity Press, 1971), pp. 28-29.

⁵New Testament instances of *thelēma* as God's will: Mt. 6:10; 7:21; 12:50; 18:14; 26:42; Mk. 3:35; Lk. 11:2; 22:42; Jn. 1:13; 4:34; 5:30; 6:38-40; 7:17; 9:31; Acts 13:22; 21:14; 22:14; Ruth 1:10; 2:18; 12:2; 15:32; 1 Cor. 1:1; 16:12 (probably); 2 Cor. 1:1; 8:5; Gal. 1:4; Eph. 1:1, 5, 9,11; 5:17; 6:6; Col. 1:1, 9; 4:12; 1 Thess. 4:3; 5:18; 2 Tim. 1:1; Heb. 10:7, 9-10, 36; 13:21; 1 Pet. 2:15; 3:17; 4:2, 19; 1 Jn. 2:17; 5:14; Rev. 4:11.

⁶New Testament instances of *boulē* as God's will (sometimes rendered *counsel* or *purpose*): Acts 2:23; 5:38-39; 13:36; 20:27; Rom. 9:19 (actually *boulēma*, a derivative noun); Eph. 1:11 (rendered *counsel; will* in this verse is *thelēma*); Heb. 6:17. Also, Lk. 7:30, which is an exception to the general usage of *boulē*.

⁷For a helpful discussion of New Testament words translated as *God's will*, see Marion Nelson, *How to Know God's Will* (Chicago: Moody Press, 1963), pp. 10-14.

⁸See Rom. 12:6; 1 Cor. 12:10, 28-29; 14:1ff; Eph. 4:11.

⁹Gerhard Friedrich, "prophētēs" in the *Theological Dictionary of the New Testament* (TDNT), Vol. VI (trans. G. W. Bromiley [Grand Rapids: Eerdmans, 1968], 829), states regarding the Greek word for prophecy: "In Paul the word has a predominantly ethical and hortatory character. It denotes teaching, admonishing and comforting, 1 Cor. 14:3, 31. The one who prophesies utters the divine call of judgment and repentance which is burdensome and tormenting to many (Rev. 11:3, 10) but which convicts others of sin and leads them to the worship of God (1 Cor. 14: 24f)."

¹⁰See Ex. 22:18; Lev. 19:26, 31; 20:6; 22:27; Deut. 18:10-11; Is. 2:6; 8:19-20; 44:25; 47:12-13; Mic. 5:12; Zech. 10:2; Mal. 3:5.

Chapter 3

¹See Gen. 49:24; Ps. 23; Ps. 79:13; Ps. 80:1; Ps. 95:7; Ps. 100:3; Is. 40: 11; Jer. 31:10; Ezek. 34, 37:24.

²William Barclay, *The Gospel of John, Daily Study Bible,* Vol. 2 (Philadelphia: Westminster Press, 1956), 68.

[3]I would refer the reader to two excellent and readable discussions of the shepherd's role in New Testament times and its implications: William Barclay, ibid., pp. 60ff; and Leon Morris, *The Gospel According to John,* New International Commentary on the New Testament, (Grand Rapids: Eerdmans, 1971), pp. 498ff.

[4]This is precisely Morris's term in describing an important aspect of the biblical picture of God as a shepherd, ibid., 498.

[5]See Barclay, *The Gospel of John,* p. 64.

[6]See, for example, Mt. 9:36; 10:6; 15:24; 18:12.

Chapter 4

[1]Jonah is the most notable exception, but the overwhelming majority of people called by God were willing to obey.

[2]Johannes Behm, "Nous," Vol. IV, TDNT, 958.

[3]George Eldon Ladd, *A Theology of the New Testament* (Grand Rapids: Eerdmans, 1974), pp. 524-25.

[4]Oliver R. Barclay, *Guidance,* 5th ed. (Downers Grove, Ill.: InterVarsity Press, 1978), p. 49.

Chapter 5

[1]C. S. Lewis, "The Efficacy of Prayer" in *The World's Last Night and Other Essays* (New York: Harcourt, Brace & World, 1959), p. 9; and "Work and Prayer" in *God in the Dock* (Grand Rapids: Eerdmans, 1970), pp. 104-107.

[2]John Calvin, *Institutes of the Christian Religion,* 3. 20. 2.

[3]Andrew Murray, *With Christ in the School of Prayer* (Old Tappan, N. J.: Revell, 1974), p. 103.

[4]Albert Barnes, *Barnes Notes on the New Testament* (Grand Rapids: Kregal Publ., 1962), p. 1356.

[5]Paul Little, *Affirming the Will of God* (Downers Grove, Ill.: InterVarsity Press, 1971), pp. 17-18.

[6]Ibid., p. 7.

[7]Paul asked Christ to reveal his will when he appeared to Paul on the Damascus road. Paul asked, "What shall I do, Lord?" (Acts 22:10).

Chapter 6

[1]R. C. Sproul, *Knowing Scripture* (Downers Grove, Ill.: InterVarsity Press, 1977).

[2]John White, *The Fight* (Downers Grove, Ill.: InterVarsity Press, 1976), pp. 157-58.

Chapter 7

[1]The verb *come* is *elthōn,* an aorist participle, which gives the sense of *having come.* The phrase *having come to you through the will of God* is introduced by *ina* ("in order that"), which most likely makes v. 32 an effect of which v. 31 is the cause. Paul seems to be saying, then, that if the conditions of v. 31 are fulfilled (his being delivered from unbelievers and

delivering the contribution to Jerusalem), he will then come to Rome in the will of God. See F. J. Leenhardt, *The Epistle to the Romans* (London: Lutterworth Press, 1961), pp. 376-77.

[2]John A. Allan, "The Will of God in Paul," in *Expository Times*, Vol. LXXII, No. 5 (1961), 145.

[3]Kenneth Pike, "God's Guidance and Your Life Work," in Joseph Bayly et al., *Essays on Guidance* (Downers Grove, Ill.: InterVarsity Press, 1968), p. 69.

[4]Ibid., pp. 69-70.

[5]Colossians 1:9 states: "We have not ceased to pray for you, asking that you may be filled with the knowledge of his will in all spiritual wisdom and understanding." Ralph Martin (*Colossians and Philemon*, New Century Bible [London: Oliphants, 1974], p. 50) notes that the prayer is really best understood as an exhortation to the Colossians. Paul is in effect telling them to "be filled with the knowledge of God's will in all spiritual wisdom and understanding." The readers, then, are being exhorted to make full use of all rational faculties to discern God's will.

Ephesians 5:15-17 states: "Look carefully then how you walk, not as unwise men but as wise, making the most of the time, because the days are evil. Therefore do not be foolish, but understand what the will of the Lord is." Paul here is giving his readers a command to be practical. "Making the most of the time" implies taking the best and most logical advantage of circumstances for the Lord's glory. "Understand" in v. 17 is the Greek term *suniete,* implying a rational process of discernment.

[6]James H. Jauncy, *Guidance by God* (Grand Rapids: Zondervan, 1969), p. 71.

Chapter 8

[1]Martin Luther, *Letters,* Luther's Works, Vol. 1 (Philadelphia: Fortress, 1963), 366-67.

[2]Dispensationalism, which is a particular form of conservative theology, divides history into several ages. Particular biblical passages are believed to apply only to particular periods. Thus, the experiences of supernatural guidance found in the New Testament are said to apply only to the apostolic age. Any claims to direct guidance by modern Christians would be considered false. In this book, I have tried to take a more moderate approach.

[3]Bob Mumford, *Take Another Look at Guidance* (Plainfield, N. J.: Logos Int., 1971), p. 127.

[4]When Paul talks about the gift of prophecy, he makes no statement to the effect that it should be thought of as a channel of guidance. There are plenty of examples of prediction in the New Testament, such as Agabus's prediction of the famine (Acts 11:28) and predictions by various New Testament writers about God's future acts in history. But with the exception of Acts 21:4, noted immediately below, there is no clear instance where someone attempted to connect prophecy with advice for

another's complex decision. And, as we note, in Acts 21:4, the one exception where this did happen, Paul did not take the advice as God's will. This is not to argue from silence that prophecy never did function as guidance in the New Testament church. But certainly if God had wanted it to be a normal channel of guidance for us today it would have been made more apparent in the New Testament. Some references to the gift of prophecy in Paul's writings are Rom. 12:6; 1 Cor. 12:10; 13:2, 9; 14:3-6, 22, 24-25, 31, 39-40. Cf. Eph. 4:11-12.

⁵I am assuming that Paul's statement in Acts 20:23 ("the Holy Spirit testifies to me in every city that imprisonment and afflictions await me") implies that this warning came through the prophecy of friends. This assumption has the support of the following commentaries: F. F. Bruce, *Commentary on the Book of Acts* (Grand Rapids: Eerdmans, 1974), p. 414; Richard B. Rackham, *The Acts of the Apostles* (London: Methuen, 1904), p. 390; Ernst Haenchen, *The Acts of the Apostles: A Commentary* (Oxford: Basil Blackwell, 1971), p. 591.

⁶Bruce, *Commentary on the Book of Acts,* p. 421.

⁷We should remember that the gift of prophecy in the New Testament refers more to teaching than to prediction. See note 9, chapter 2.

⁸Michael Harper, *Prophecy: A Gift for the Body of Christ* (Plainfield, N.J.: Logos Int., 1970), pp. 26-27.

Chapter 9

¹The phrase *still small voice* comes from 1 Kings 19:12. There is, however, no indication in the passage that the "still small voice" has any reference to inward guidance. It seems that Elijah heard God's audible voice (vv. 13-18). The term is employed in the passage to contrast God's voice with the wind, earthquake and fire immediately preceding.

²Acts references to the inspiration of the Holy Spirit are 8:26, 39; 10: 19-20; 11:28; 13:2; 15:28; 16:6-7; 19:21; 20:22-23; 21:4, 11-14.

³This does not mean that we are supposed to ignore guilt feelings when making complex decisions. To do so would be both spiritual and psychological suicide. But at the same time we will seldom make a major decision without experiencing some guilt feelings or some sense of fear that perhaps we are choosing the wrong alternative. This is the natural response of the human psyche. If we waited for absolute peace in every major decision, we would be paralyzed. Fortunately Paul is not laying down such a difficult commandment.

⁴Barclay, *Guidance,* p. 40.

Chapter 11

¹Charles E. Hummel, *Fire in the Fireplace: Contemporary Charismatic Renewal* (Downers Grove, Ill.: InterVarsity Press, 1978). This superb treatment of the subject covers a wide range of topics related to spiritual gifts.

²Ibid., pp. 168-69.

[3]Ibid., p. 130.

[4]Ibid., p. 228.

[5]Again, a helpful comment from Hummel: "Therefore, the believer does not struggle to discover his or her individual gift and then wonder where to use it. Instead the Christian participates in the body and, sensitive to the needs of others, trusts the sovereign Spirit to manifest whatever gifts will meet the needs of the community. The community benefits from and controls the exercise of gifts." Ibid., p. 171.

[6]The term *bishop* in this passage should be understood as meaning "overseer"; it does not have the ecclesiastical connotations of the contemporary term. *Bishop (episkopos)* and *elder (presbyteros)* were in New Testament times alternative names for the same officer (see Tit. 1:5, 7; Acts 20:17, 28), the first term indicating function or duty and the second, dignity or status. Each local congregation had several persons functioning as overseers. (A.M. Stibbs, "The Pastoral Epistles," in *The New Bible Commentary: Revised,* eds. D. Guthrie and J. A. Motyer [Grand Rapids: Eerdmans, 1970], p. 1171.) See also Titus 1:5-9 for another Pauline example of qualifications for church leadership, and Acts 6:2-5 for an example from Luke of qualifications required for a deacon.

[7]Joseph is exalted to high positions in Egypt because of his gifts (Gen. 39ff). Aaron is chosen to be Moses' mouthpiece because he could speak well (Ex. 4:14-16). Moses' choice of men to be rulers under him is based purely on consideration of their ability (Ex. 18:21), as is his choice of persons to make Aaron's garments (Ex. 28:3) and of people to construct the temple (Ex. 31:1-11; 35:10, 30—36:2). Joshua was chosen as Moses' successor because of the spirit in him (Num. 27:18). Gideon chose the men for his small army on the basis of their courageousness (Judg. 7:2-3). Saul brings David into his court because of his musical ability (1 Sam. 16:14-23) and hires Hiram (1 Kings 7:13-14) and Jeroboam (1 Kings 11:28) for special service because of their talents. David in choosing his officers from the Gadites put "the lesser over a hundred and the greater over a thousand" (1 Chron. 12:14), and he made Chenaniah director of music "for he understood it" (1 Chron. 15:22).

Chapter 12

[1]Martin Luther, *The Sermon on the Mount,* Luther's Works, Vol. 21 (St. Louis: Concordia, 1956), 239.

Chapter 13

[1]See also Prov. 13:10, 18, 20; 15:31-32; 17:10; 19:25.

Chapter 14

[1]Quoted by J. Oswald Sanders, *Spiritual Leadership* (Chicago: Moody Press, 1967), p. 113.

Appendix

[1]Bill Gothard, subsection "Chain-of-Command" in section "Family" in *Institute in Basic Youth Conflicts* (LaGrange, Ill.: Institute in Basic Youth Conflicts, 1969 and Campus Teams Inc., 1968).

[2]See F. F. Bruce and E. K. Simpson, *Commentary on the Epistles to the Ephesians and the Colossians,* New International Commentary on the New Testament (Grand Rapids: Eerdmans, 1957), p. 291.

[3]Thomas K. Abbott, *The Epistles to the Ephesians and to the Colossians,* International Critical Commentary (New York: Scribner's, 1903), p. 176.

[4]John Eadie, *A Commentary on the Greek Text of the Epistle of Paul to the Colossians* (Edinburgh: T. & T. Clark, 1884), p. 255.

[5]See Eduard Lohse, *A Commentary on the Epistles to the Colossians and to Philemon* Hermeneia (Philadelphia: Fortress, 1971), p. 159. This conclusion is highly probable on the basis of Eph. 6:4, where Paul certainly employs *ta tekna* with the same intended meaning as in 6:1, and he states, "Fathers, do not provoke your children to anger, but *bring them up* in the discipline and instruction of the Lord," indicating that he has in mind an adolescent dependency relationship in this use of *tekna.*

[6]A scholarly treatment of the subject is given by Paul K. Jewett, *MAN as Male and Female* (Grand Rapids: Eerdmans, 1975). He advocates the position that the commands on marital authority are not binding on modern Christians. A good argument for the traditional interpretation is given by George W. Knight III, *The New Testament Teaching on the Role Relationship of Men and Women* (Grand Rapids: Baker Book House, 1977).

[7]Willis Peter DeBoer, *The Imitation of Paul: An Exegetical Study* (Amsterdam: Vrige Univ., 1962), p. vi.

[8]W. E. Vine, *An Expository Dictionary of New Testament Words,* Vol. III (Old Tappen, N. J. : Revell, 1966), 124.

[9]The verb *obey* is coupled with the verb *submit,* which in the Greek is *upeikete.* Unlike the verb for *obey (peithesthe)* this word is not used elsewhere in the New Testament, so it is more difficult to determine its precise meaning. It is perhaps intended to give depth to *obey,* suggesting that one should not only strive to agree with a leader's (reasonable) directives but should also put these into practice when one is persuaded they are valid. Again, there is no evidence that this word implies compliance with a leader's counsel in the area of complex decisions.

About the Author

M. Blaine Smith is currently director of Nehemiah Ministries, Inc. He holds the bachelor of science degree from Georgetown University, the master of divinity degree from Wesley Theological Seminary, and the doctor of ministry degree from Fuller Theological Seminary. He was formerly director of a contemporary music ministry called "Sons of Thunder," and served as assistant minister of Memorial Presbyterian Church in St. Louis.

Nehemiah Ministries, Inc., is a resource organization providing general interest seminars to churches and pastoral services to Christian performing artists. Smith has developed a seminar on knowing God's will which is designed to help college-age and high-school young people work through major life decisions. This workshop is a part of the resources available through Nehemiah Ministries. For further information or to contact the author, write Nehemiah Ministries, P.O. Box 448, Damascus, MD 20872.